The Improvising Teacher

The Improvising Teacher offers a radical reconceptualisation of improvisation as a fundamental element of teacher expertise. Drawing on theories of improvisation and expertise alongside empirical research, the book argues that teacher expertise is essentially improvisatory.

The book provides a theoretical model for teacher expertise that is relevant internationally and illustrates the nature of advanced practice in a global classroom through case studies of expert teachers in England. It makes a theoretical and conceptual case to support the argument for the improvising teacher as a prototype model of expert practice. Sorensen draws on critical studies in improvisation and the study of expertise and expert practice and argues that now more than ever, teachers must be flexible, creative and skilled in adaptation. Providing a critical evaluation on how to approach the professional development of the improvising teacher, the book outlines how the improvising teacher signifies a broader cultural shift in the way we understand teaching and teacher professionalism.

This book will be essential reading for academics, researchers and postgraduate students in the fields of teacher education, professional practice, professional development and critical studies in improvisation. It will also be highly relevant for teacher educators who are attempting to understand, research and promote teacher expertise and teacher autonomy in education across the world.

Nick Sorensen is Emeritus Professor of Education, Bath Spa University, UK.

Routledge Research in Education

This series aims to present the latest research from right across the field of education. It is not confined to any particular area or school of thought and seeks to provide coverage of a broad range of topics, theories and issues from around the world.

A Retrospective Study of a Dialogic Elementary Classroom
Understanding Long-Term Impacts of Discursive Pedagogies
Lynn Astarita Gatto

Thinking with Stephen J. Ball
Lines of Flight in Education
Maria Tamboukou

A History of Inspiration through Metaphors of Learning
The Height of Teaching
Robert Nelson

Relational Aspects of Parental Involvement to Support Educational Outcomes
Parental Communication, Expectations, and Participation for Student Success
Edited by William Jeynes

Navigating Precarity in Educational Contexts
Reflection, Pedagogy, and Activism for Change
Edited by Karen Monkman, Ann Frkovich, and Amira Proweller

The Improvising Teacher
Reconceptualising Pedagogy, Expertise and Professionalism
Nick Sorensen

For more information about this series, please visit: www.routledge.com/Routledge-Research-in-Education/book-series/SE0393

The Improvising Teacher
Reconceptualising Pedagogy, Expertise and Professionalism

Nick Sorensen

LONDON AND NEW YORK

First published 2023
by Routledge
4 Park Square, Milton Park, Abingdon, Oxon OX14 4RN

and by Routledge
605 Third Avenue, New York, NY 10158

Routledge is an imprint of the Taylor & Francis Group, an informa business

© 2023 Nick Sorensen

The right of Nick Sorensen to be identified as author of this work has been asserted in accordance with sections 77 and 78 of the Copyright, Designs and Patents Act 1988.

All rights reserved. No part of this book may be reprinted or reproduced or utilised in any form or by any electronic, mechanical, or other means, now known or hereafter invented, including photocopying and recording, or in any information storage or retrieval system, without permission in writing from the publishers.

Trademark notice: Product or corporate names may be trademarks or registered trademarks, and are used only for identification and explanation without intent to infringe.

British Library Cataloguing-in-Publication Data
A catalogue record for this book is available from the British Library

Library of Congress Cataloging-in-Publication Data
A catalog record has been requested for this book

ISBN: 9781032121253 (hbk)
ISBN: 9781032121260 (pbk)
ISBN: 9781003223207 (ebk)

DOI: 10.4324/9781003223207

Typeset in Bembo
by KnowledgeWorks Global Ltd.

To Sandra

Contents

List of figures	ix
List of tables	x
Foreword by Theresa Robbins Dudeck	xi
Preface	xiii
Acknowledgements	xiv
1 Introduction	1

PART I
Theoretical and conceptual foundations — 13

2 Understanding improvisation: A working definition and philosophical assumptions	15
3 Understanding expertise and the lexicon of advanced professional practice in teaching	34
4 Understanding professionalism and the discourses of advanced professional practice	47

PART II
The empirical research: The improvisational nature of teacher expertise — 61

5 The impact of school culture on the development of advanced professional practice	63
6 Teacher perceptions of expertise and improvisation	77
7 The improvising teacher as a prototype of advanced professional practice	87
8 The social construction of the improvising teacher	98

PART III
Implications for practice   113

9 Towards a long-term framework for the professional
   development of the improvising teacher   115

10 Afterword: The improvising teacher in
   the COVID-19 present   131

   References   146
   Index   154

List of figures

5.1	A model of school culture	76
7.1	A grounded theory of the ecology of advanced professional practice	88
7.2	Developing the improvising teacher	97
8.1	The school ecology: structure, power and culture	99
8.2	The improvising teacher: three phases of empowerment	110
9.1	The authorised teacher	118
9.2	The three dispositions of the improvisation mindset and the four skills of improvisational teaching	129
10.1	PowerPoint slide as a gateway to JamBoard	139

List of tables

2.1	The 11 key characteristics of improvisational practice	25
2.2	A working definition of improvisation	28
2.3	Commonalities between social constructionism, critical theory and transformative teleology	33
3.1	Summary of Dreyfus and Dreyfus (1986) five stages of skill acquisition	39
3.2	Summary of Sternberg and Horvath (1995) expert teaching prototype	45
5.1	Summary of experience of headteachers interviewed	68
6.1	'Headline' statements summarising what the term 'expert teaching' means.	79
6.2	'Headline' statements grouped under the three themes of teacher expertise	80
7.1	Comparison between the improvising teacher and Smith and Strahan (2004)	93
8.1	Analysis of teacher-learner relationships and power structures in relation to Habermas's three kinds of knowledge	105
9.1	Comparison of relationships between the improvising teacher, Dreyfus and Dreyfus (1986), Sorensen and Coombs (2010a) and Bruner's teacher perceptions of students.	123

Foreword

In 2016, I was teaching a variety of improvisation courses – for actors, future teachers, leaders – in both the theatre and graduate education programs at a private university in California. Leslie Odom Jr., fresh from his Tony Award win for *Hamilton*, visited our campus and gave this advice to our students and faculty: College 'is the place you should fall on your face and your teachers should encourage you and say 'Great, try something else, try it again. I love that you went so far you tipped over'.

In March 2020, when the pandemic forced us into lockdown and teachers everywhere found themselves suddenly shifting their courses online, one thing became clear: colleges had not trained teachers to be resilient, to tip over and buoyantly get up and try again. Some teachers panicked, others gave up, many slowly and begrudgingly transitioned.

But a hearty bunch seemed to handle the onslaught of curveballs with agility. They not only adapted more easily to online facilitation, they viewed the disruption as an opportunity to innovate their courses and to try new modalities for more equitable, integrative learning. Consciously or unconsciously, these teachers were applying an improvisation mindset to the moment.

The benefits of this improvisation mindset go well beyond moments of crisis. Having an improvisation mindset means meeting every moment in life, within and beyond the classroom, like a good improviser. Good improvisers are adept at balancing between structure (e.g., rules, principles, lesson plans) and spontaneity (going off-script). They accept everything as an offer (even mistakes), commit to building on those offers, listen wholeheartedly, engage authentically, and embrace change as inevitable, usually with grace and often with joy.

This book is about how expert teachers are improvising teachers. Through their stories, Nick Sorensen shows us how improvisation and an improvisation mindset are fundamental to their teaching. The book also underscores that these aptitudes weren't learned in college programs. These skills were honed on the job, over years of regular, intentional practice and reflection.

Sorensen makes a strong case for encouraging artful, skilled improvisation in the classroom and in teacher training programs. He draws on decades of field and applied research to establish a relationship between improvisation and teacher expertise. Both the improviser and the improvising teacher follow intuitive impulses. And like the best improvisers, expert teachers often make what they do look effortless. But the skills they apply to create exciting, spontaneous experiences in the classroom have been ripening for years. All the teachers you will read about in this book believe their improvisation mindset and muscles will continue to develop over a long journey of learning, discovering, and transforming. All take bold risks, tip over, try something else, tip over, and try again.

The motif of 'teaching as a journey' weaves throughout. Keith Johnstone, a master teacher and pioneer of improvisation and pedagogical methods adopted across disciplines worldwide, once told me that teaching, more than anything else, is the summit for him. Despite his mastery, he claims he doesn't know how to do it yet – because the path to the summit is everchanging, always challenging, and a continuous mystery.

The teachers in this study are reticent to be called 'expert teachers' because, I imagine, they feel like Keith – every day offers new challenges that require them to do things they don't yet know how to do! Well of course they do, but a wonderful humility radiates from every improvising teacher we meet. This humility stems from their belief that true 'teacher expertise' is never fully attained but rather something to continuously strive for, and success in the classroom is always dependent on the success of their student partners.

In the theatre improvisation world, a key tenet is 'to make your partner look good'. It reminds players to focus on others, to give the other player whatever they need in the moment, to find out what inspires or engages them, and to fully support the team to create an ideal climate for collaborative creation.

The improvising teacher applies this tenet to create an engaged classroom in ways that empower students, unleash their imaginations, and intensify their desire to learn. Above all, the improvising teacher believes that all students of all abilities can succeed and dismisses any one-size-fits-all approach.

Whether you are just beginning or continuing your unique teaching journey, as you navigate the challenging, unpredictable, exciting path to the summit, I hope you embrace and develop the improvising teacher within you. This book can help show you the way.

Theresa Robbins Dudeck, PhD
Theatre scholar-practitioner, expert in improvisation and applied improvisation
Co-founder of the Global Improvisation Initiative
Adjunct Professor, Portland State University, USA

Preface

Writing this book has provided me with the opportunity to give a full account of a research project undertaken to explore the relationship between improvisation and expertise for teachers. Additionally it has allowed me to re-engage with ideas that had been developed both prior to and also subsequent to the research. In contemplating the overall design for this book I realised that it would be logical to bring all of these ideas and concepts together in order to be able to explore and articulate the relationship between them.

Early work on the authorised teacher (Sorensen and Coombs, 2010a) and a long-term framework for teacher development (Sorensen and Coombs, 2010b) seemed to complement the arguments for the improvising teacher. More recent writings have explored the implications of the research findings within specific contexts: the craft of teaching musical improvisation improvisationally (Sorensen, 2021a), the importance of the applied improvisation mindset (Sorensen, 2021b) and the development of expertise in Higher Education teaching (Sorensen, 2022).

Bringing these ideas and concepts together in one volume offers a synoptic account of the work that I have done over the past 40 years considering the meaning and value of improvisation and its importance for teachers. The process of writing this book brought about a realisation of how my thoughts have changed over this time and this has resulted in the development of some ideas and the revision of others.

I hope that this book will provide a greater understanding of the creative agency of teachers and the positive impact that this has upon students. Furthermore I hope that it encourages a collective effort by teachers, school leaders and policy makers to create cultures that are conducive to improvisation and the shared development of expertise.

Nick Sorensen, December 2021

Acknowledgements

To begin with I must give my most grateful thanks to the teachers who participated in this study. I am grateful for their generosity in allowing me to interview them, observe their teaching and for sharing their insights into what made them such incredible teachers. Likewise I would want to thank the headteachers who, as gatekeepers, enabled this project to take place and for their contribution to understanding how school culture nurtures great teaching.

Steven Coombs, Jill White and Stephen Ward gave valuable guidance and support with the research project. Their critical engagement and advice was crucially important and I thank them for their time, patience and wisdom.

Along the way I have received advice, encouragement and support from many colleagues and friends. Particular thanks are due to Kyriaki Anagnostopoulou, Pam Burnard, John Clarke, Andy Goodwyn, Nick Gould, Helen King, Fiona Maine, Roisin Ni Mhochain, Tanya Ovenden-Hope, Rod Paton, Sandra Porter, Chris Wilkins and Mark Wilson. I am also grateful to my colleagues in the School of Education at Bath Spa University who have contributed to the many discussions that have helped shape and clarify my thinking.

1 Introduction

Introduction

Anecdotal evidence, supported by common sense knowledge, tells us that one of the characteristics of great teachers is that they have the ability to improvise. In fact most teachers when asked if they think that improvisation is important to their practice will not only say 'yes' but will then be able to supply a story about how some of their best teaching occurred when the premeditated lesson plan was abandoned. The following is an actual and typical example:

> *I used to plan everything, down to the last minute. I went into a class one day and, I don't know what it was exactly, but the whole group was not in the mood for learning so I just stood up and I literally picked up my printed lesson plan and walked to the bin, dropped it in it and said 'so what are we going to talk about today?' That one little thing scared the life out of me as I realised I would be winging it but I also had trust in myself ... and it was a brilliant session and they actually ended up learning quite a lot because we just pulled out from what they talked about various bits that I hoped they would learn anyway. It was quite a powerful experience from my perspective and the students.*
>
> (Roisin)

When a teacher chooses to improvise, or is forced to do so, it can lead to some of their best experiences as an educator. They come alive as they step 'into the moment', respond to the unexpected and gain confidence in their ability to engage with and relate to students. Out of necessity they draw upon their full range of professional experiences and who they are as a person. These anecdotes are important because they offer first-hand accounts of those precise moments when 'good' teachers become 'great'. They provide a portal into the essence of teacher expertise and also suggest that many of the things that teachers are required to do can seem to hold them back from being the best they can be.

Stories such as Roisin's instigated this enquiry into the improvisational nature of teaching and led to asking questions about the relationship

DOI: 10.4324/9781003223207-1

between improvisation and expertise and what it means to be professional. Improvisational practice is the reality for many teachers; it is a core skill. Yet, although this is a common understanding for many teachers, learning about improvisation is rarely included in initial teacher education courses or continuing professional development programmes. So how is it that one of the defining characteristics of advanced professional practice is seldom talked about?

There are many reasons for this. Accountability structures in schools and colleges privilege the importance of lesson planning and lesson outcomes and this can discourage teachers from talking about improvisation. Many teacher development programmes are based on standardised pedagogies that are derived from 'best practice'. This occurs in spite of the fact that evidence suggests that what works in one context may not be effective in another. Furthermore improvisation is a misunderstood and problematic phenomenon that can mean many different things to different people. Imbued with negative as well as positive connotations, definitions of improvisation are often contradictory and confusing. Consequently there is a deficiency in the language and concepts that make it possible to talk about improvisation within the context of teaching. For over a decade now education systems across the world have concurred that 'the main driver of the variation in student learning at school is the quality of the teachers' (Barber and Mourshed, 2007: 12) and consequently 'the world's best performing school systems make great teaching their "north star"' (Auguste et al., 2010: 5). This study acknowledges these viewpoints whilst recognising the global challenge of recruiting and retaining teachers. The concept of the improvising teacher is offered in response to the perennial questions of how 'good' teachers can be transformed into 'great' teachers and how they can be encouraged to stay in the profession.

The Improvising Teacher: Reconceptualising Pedagogy, Expertise and Professionalism aims to transform the common-sense knowledge held about improvisation and the advanced professional practice of teaching by drawing on empirical research and a systematic critical examination of the concepts that inform improvisational practice. The empirical research was undertaken to explore the relationship between improvisation and expertise and data was obtained from a comparative case study of seven outstanding teachers working in secondary schools in the UK.

The research findings conclude that there is a reciprocal relationship between improvisation and expertise: the ability to improvise is a facet of expertise and expert practice is fundamentally improvisational. The impact of school culture on the development of expert practice is also recognised and this leads to understanding expertise as a social construction. Advanced professional practice (expert practice) is expressed through the concept of the improvising teacher. Although the research looked at a small sample of secondary teachers in the UK, these findings have relevance for teachers in all phases of education and in many other countries.

The concept of the improvising teacher is important because it provides new and unique insights into the way advanced professional practice is understood. It affirms the significance of improvisation-based pedagogies that are grounded in expertise and are socially constructed. The theoretical and conceptual frameworks derived from the empirical data provide a rationale for accepting common sense knowledge about improvisational teaching and provide the basis for a reconceptualisation of pedagogy, expertise and professionalism.

Establishing a mutual relationship between improvisation and expertise challenges long-held assumptions about teacher professionalism and what is considered to be professional practice. Acknowledging the improvising teacher demands a reconceptualisation of professionalism that takes into account authenticity, the authorisation to make professional judgements, and acknowledges teacher autonomy. It also suggests alternative approaches to initial teacher education and subsequent professional development by privileging approaches that value creativity and collaborative working. This book concludes with a framework for the long-term development to support and develop the improvising teacher.

The concept of the improvising teacher, and the issues that arise from it, has an international relevance. There is a global interest in finding ways to improve teacher quality and this is now informed by a growing interest in the research into teacher expertise. Improvisational teaching is receiving considerable attention in many countries and is an expanding field of research, theory and practice, especially in the USA, Canada and Scandinavia. The ability to improvise fosters creativity, autonomy and adaptability: essential characteristics that are sought in all teachers and that have a positive impact on teacher satisfaction, which in turn supports teacher retention (a considerable and growing international concern).

The next section of this chapter offers a first-person account of the rationale and the motivation to undertake this research into improvisation within the context of teaching.

Rationale for the research

The motivation to undertake a research project to study the improvisatory nature of expert teaching has been driven by three personal interests. The first of these is my long-standing interest in improvisation as a musician (I am a jazz saxophonist) and as a researcher. My academic interest in improvisation began in the mid-1980s when I enrolled for the Independent Studies MA in Education at the University of Sussex. This provided me with an opportunity to explore improvisation as a significant and identifiable mode of creativity that could be found in all the Arts, not just in music. The research that I undertook for my Master's degree was multi-disciplinary and included a critical evaluation of my practice as a drama teacher, a musicological investigation of the improvisatory practices of six musicians representing different genres of music and a theoretical dissertation that explored the value of improvisation for arts educators.

Having completed this award I became very aware that there was so much more to be said about improvisation particularly in the context of 'everyday life'. Understanding the improvisatory nature of the social world seemed to be important particularly in relation to studying the ways in which schools and educational processes function as social entities. This led me to explore a range of interrelated theoretical perspectives. The metaphor of 'the jazz band', for example, provided insights into the improvisatory nature of organisations (Hatch, 1997) and has informed our understanding of leadership (Newton, 2004), schools (Stoll et al., 2003) and even the meaning of life (Eagleton, 2008). Piaget's (1990) view of intelligence (what you use when you don't know what to do) highlights the improvisatory nature of learning, an idea that has been explicitly developed to inform metacognitive approaches to pedagogy (Claxton, 1999, 2002; Deakin Crick et al., 2004; Deakin Crick, 2006).

We improvise everyday in our social lives whenever we engage in conversation; dialogue is very much at the heart of the educational process. Social constructionists acknowledge a reality that is created through discussion and description and this informs their view of learning.

Based on notions of intersubjectivity and the social nature of learning (Vygotsky, 1978) they give attention to the dialogic nature of the social world. The word 'dialogic', often accompanied by an attribution of Bakhtin, is applied to the study of educational dialogue which, as Wegerif (2008) points out, 'always implies at least two voices (and) assumes underlying difference rather than identity' (348). Constructivist and dialogic pedagogies acknowledge that the unpredictability of multiple completing voices make discussion a uniquely effective teaching tool. These approaches are deemed as being 'fundamentally improvisational' (Sawyer, 2004: 190) because if the classroom is scripted and controlled by the teacher, then students are unable to engage in the co-construction of knowledge. The improvisational assumptions implicit within these theories of learning and pedagogy suggest that the improvisatory nature of teaching is an area that deserves research.

The second area of interest, which is derived from the first, came from my professional role supporting the continuing professional development of teachers, initially as an independent education consultant and then as a senior lecturer in higher education (HE) leading a professional masters programme (PMP). My experience of engaging in this work caused me to ask questions about what the goal of professional development ought to be and what we should call 'good' teaching (Coffield and Edwards, 2009). I recognised that there was a need to theorise what advanced professional practice should look like given that such a theoretical framework for long-term teacher development did not exist (Hoban, 2002).

This led to the development of a four-phase model of professional practice (Sorensen and Coombs, 2010a) articulating the progress from Phase One (a teacher-centred classroom) to Phase Four (a learner-centred classroom supported by creative pedagogies). The fourth phase describes a pedagogy whereby students are actively engaged in a dialogic process of learning that is facilitated and supported by the teacher. This is a mode of teaching that relies on the ability to improvise and respond to the needs of students.

This process of pedagogic advancement is augmented and supported by a reconceptualisation of professional status articulated by the concept of 'the authorised teacher' (Sorensen and Coombs, 2010b). The 'authorised teacher' acknowledges a professional autonomy that is grounded in critical professional practice and defined by three related concepts: 'authenticity', 'authorisation' and 'authoring'. This view of advanced professional practice sees professional values as being generated by and situated within communities of learning that employ reflective and critical practices to support professional development. The four-phase model of professional development and the concept of 'the authorised teacher' are outlined in detail in Chapter 9.

The third area of interest that informed the research was instigated by the debates that arose out of the educational reforms initiated by the UK coalition government from 2010 to 2015. Heralded in the White Paper 'The Importance of Teaching' (DfE, 2010), these reforms built upon and extended the neoliberal policies introduced by the 1988 Education Act and accelerated the marketisation of the education system. Greater autonomy was given to schools and headteachers, the 'middle tier' of local authorities that had responsibility for educational provision was dismantled, schools were converted into academies and multi-academy trusts (MATS) were established. The National Curriculum was revised, with preference given to traditional academic subjects and rote learning. A hundred academics, in a letter to the *Independent* newspaper in 2013, challenged these reforms on the grounds that they would not support a child's ability to solve problems, develop critical understanding and act creatively. In response to this letter Michael Gove, the then Secretary of State for Education, branded them as 'enemies of promise' (Gove, 2013).

For the Coalition government 'the first, and most important, lesson is that no education system can be better than the quality of its teachers' (DfE, 2010: 3). This view, which was driven by comparison with 'international competitors' (3), references the McKinsey Report 'Closing the talent gap: attracting and retaining top-third graduates to careers in teaching' (Auguste et al. 2010) that prioritises the effectiveness of the classroom teacher. 'The Importance of Teaching' declares that:

> We do not have a strong enough focus on what is proven to be the most effective practice in teacher education and development. We know that teachers learn best from other professionals and that an 'open classroom' culture is vital: observing teaching and being observed, having the opportunity to plan, prepare, reflect and teach with other teachers.
> (DfE, 2010: 19)

These reforms, and the debates that surrounded them, stimulated my interest to examine classroom practice in order to gain a greater understanding of 'effective' teaching. This view was deliberately built from a 'bottom up' perspective as opposed to the 'top down' policy-led approaches outlined in 'The Importance of Teaching'.

These three areas of interest (the improvisational nature of social contexts, my work with the continuing professional development of teachers and the ideological educational reforms promoted in 'The Importance of Teaching') generated a number of questions about the advanced professional practice of teachers: what does it look like, how is it facilitated and supported, what do teachers have to say about this? One of the principle aims of the research was to bring the voices of teachers into this debate in order that they can make a contribution to this discourse. This book presents the findings of this study alongside theoretical perspectives that inform the ways in which the agency of teachers can be valued and developed in order to promote new approaches to the development of expertise and professional respect.

The necessity for this work was reinforced during the summer of 2021 when the UK's Conservative Government instigated a market review of initial teacher training. The outcomes from the review were presented in *Delivering World-Class Teacher Development* (DfE, 2021) as a radical reform of teacher training and professional development. The key elements of the reform are the establishment of an Institute of Teaching, a new approach to the provision of Initial Teacher Training (including the *de facto* extension of the Newly Qualified Teacher status from one to two years before the award of Qualified Teacher Status) and the delivery of an Early Careers Framework via a very small number of providers (Ovenden-Hope, 2022).

The proposed curriculum for the training of teachers will be closely informed by governmental thinking, and the structures for delivering the new reforms have side-lined the involvement of universities, who have played a long and significant role in the education of teachers. Considerable concerns about these reforms resulted in the issues relating to the recruitment and education of new teachers, and the role of universities, being debated in the House of Lords (the second chamber of the UK Parliament that plays a crucial role in examining bills, questioning government action and investigating public policy). The substance of that debate (Hansard, 2021) brought to light arguments that pertain to and are central to this book.

Both sides of the debate acknowledged that teachers are vitally important members of society and that there is nothing as important as teacher education and retention, this being the profession that creates all other professions. Teacher quality was noted as the single most important factor in improving outcomes with schools for young people and children, and the COVID-19 pandemic has increased the awareness and understanding of educational disadvantage.

The differences that emerged were over the nature of teaching as a profession, and these differing views informed whether the government's reforms were to be supported or opposed. This debate is the latest manifestation of long-term tensions that exist regarding teaching as a profession, tensions that to a greater or lesser extent are found in education systems throughout the world.

The views that support these reforms of teacher education perceive teaching as a craft that comprises a general, easily replicated sequence of activities, derived from a limited and set evidence base. They argue that the teaching profession is best regulated through the principles of the market economy in which external, top-down, ideologically driven initiatives control what is taught and how it is taught. The training of teachers is best done 'on the job' with advanced professional practice based on an essentialist understanding that the qualities and skills of 'great' teachers are determined, homogeneous and bounded. Teacher quality is determined through competencies, accountability and inspection processes and government policy.

The alternative viewpoint regards teaching as a complex relational practice derived from an intellectual and academic education in order that teachers are able, and trusted, to make professional judgements according to the specific contexts in which they are working. Professional development is viewed from a non-essentialist perspective: dynamic, heterogeneous, changeable and with blurred boundaries. The acquisition of advanced professional practice is a long-term process in which expertise is developed through critical reflection supported by communities of practice. Quality is determined by situated understandings of 'what works best' within specific contexts informed by the autonomous professional judgements of teachers supported by evidence.

This book is designed to provide the concepts and the language to support a complex and relational perspective of teaching drawing on empirical evidence. The aim is to support those teachers, teacher educators, mentors and others involved in education and professional development that hold a belief in the importance of trusting professional judgements and the value of autonomy. It is important to acknowledge the rich educational benefits for students of being taught by professionals that are skilled in adaptability, dialogic teaching and creative resourcefulness. This book reaches out to a profession that not only values improvising teachers but also understands why they are important.

Overview of chapters

The book is structured in three parts and an outline of each section along with an overview of each chapter is included here as a guide to readers. The first part of the book outlines the theoretical and conceptual foundations for understanding teacher improvisation and the ways in which pedagogy, expertise and professionalism are reconceptualised.

Chapter 2 considers the concept of improvisation as a global and universal phenomenon that is dependent on culture and context for its meaning. Consequently it is not possible to provide a single definition that covers all aspects and examples of improvised activity and this has resulted in improvisation becoming a complex and contested term that embraces a wide range of meanings and practices, many of which are conflicting and contradictory. This accounts for the problems that arise when talking about improvisation as there are a proliferation of both positive and negative views concerning its meaning and value. Literature on improvisation predominantly is concerned with artistic contexts and it is these examples that enable us to understand the improvisations that occur within the social world of the 'everyday'. Rejecting a dualistic position (e.g. contrasting improvisation with composition) this chapter offers a historical and cultural overview. Starting with Aristotle (*The Poetics*) and moving through Enlightenment and Romantic understandings to Modernist and post-modern/ecological views, this approach leads to eschewing a simple definition in favour of a statement that incorporates a field of meanings drawing on the different views that have emerged from the historical overview. The chapter concludes by outlining a range of theoretical perspectives that help to understand improvisational practice and provides a working definition that informs subsequent arguments. Pedagogy is reconceptualised as being a fundamentally improvisational practice.

Chapter 3 looks at the value of viewing the advanced professional practice of teachers through the lens of expertise and expert performance. It begins by outlining the problematic nature of the language that is used to describe the advanced professional practice of teachers and makes the case for looking at the professional development of teachers through the lens of expertise and expert performance. A critical overview is given of theories of expertise that are particularly relevant to the field of education and a distinction is made between a knowledge-based view and a practice-based view of expertise.

This book takes the latter approach, acknowledging that expertise in teaching is best acquired through practice-based approaches (as opposed to theoretical approaches). Particular attention is given to the importance of intuition and tacit knowledge in order to emphasise the improvisatory nature of expert practice. At this point the chapter brings together the working definition of improvisation and theories of expertise to provide a theoretical justification for the concept of the improvising teacher.

Chapter 4 explores how the concept of the improvising teacher raises challenging questions about the nature of professionalism and the expectations made of teachers. The chapter argues that accepting improvisation as a valid and desirable professional attribute needs to be located within an appropriate understanding of professionalism, one that acknowledges the necessity of being able to make autonomous professional judgements. The problematic issues of the nature of professionalism and the changing views of teaching as a profession are outlined and placed in a critical perspective by comparing notions of professionalism from a variety of international contexts. Different discourses to describe advanced professional practice are identified according to the extent they are influenced by managerialist or democratic principles.

The second part of the book presents the findings from empirical research undertaken to investigate the improvisational nature of teacher expertise. Drawing on interviews with headteachers and expert teachers along with observations of expert practice, the research provides strong evidence for the significance of 'the improvising teacher' as an expression of advanced professional practice. The chapters in part two engage with the findings from two perspectives: a cultural perspective and an individual perspective.

Chapter 5 provides a brief summary of the research design and methodology along with an explanation of how constant comparative methods of analysis were used to draw out themes from the data in order to construct a grounded theory of the ecology of advanced professional practice (Charmaz, 2006) that identifies teacher expertise as a social construction. Interviews with the headteachers who participated in the research demonstrate the importance of school culture (and how they shape it) and the significance they give to teacher autonomy, expertise and improvisation. The chapter concludes with some observations on subcultures and the significance that they have within the ecology of a school.

Having established the vital importance of social context to the development of teacher expertise Chapter 6 considers the improvisational nature of teacher expertise from the teachers' perspectives drawing on data derived from interviews and lesson observations.

Two themes are explored. The first is concerned with what the teachers say (using data drawn from interviews) and explores the views they hold on expertise, improvisation and the priorities that they place on dialogic teaching and the relational aspect of teaching. The second is concerned with what they do (based on evidence gained from classroom observations). This chapter privileges the teachers' voice, providing illuminating insights into the ways in which expertise is understood and displayed in practice.

Three core practices are identified as significant aspects of their expertise: the way that they were able to build positive relationships with students across the ability range, their dialogic teaching and the ability to create of a culture of learning, a personalised lifeworld within their classrooms. The lifeworld of the classroom was founded on climate setting principles (determined by the teacher through non-negotiable routines and expectations) and a culture of learning that was co-constructed with the students, reflecting their knowledge of the students as individuals and reciprocated by appropriate personal insights into the teacher as a 'real person'.

Chapter 7 presents a theoretical model of an ecology of advanced professional practice. This conceptual map offers some conclusions about the nature of teacher expertise. These are that 'a teacher with expertises' is a preferable term to 'the expert teacher'; the range of expertises that teachers have means that whilst they will have much in common they are not necessarily the same and that teacher expertise is socially constructed. This leads to claims that support the argument for seeing the improvising teacher as a model for advanced professional practice. The relationship between improvisation and expertise is explored drawing on further evidence from the empirical research, and the chapter concludes with a conceptual model of the improvising teacher.

Chapter 8 continues to examine the findings of the research theoretically, taking an organisational perspective in order to provide insights into the social construction of the improvising teacher. The school is viewed as a complex ecology shaped by the interrelationship between structure, culture and power.

Building on Sternberg and Horvath's (1995) non-essentialist view of the expert teacher, informed by the idea of a 'prototype', the context of the school is seen as a significant variable. Examples are given of the ways in which specific and situated examples of teacher expertise are informed, and formed, through a dynamic and interrelated ecology.

Part three of the book considers the implications for practice of the theory and the empirical research findings within an international context. The implications of the research findings are developed in two key areas.

In Chapter 9 the theoretical foundations presented in part one and the findings of the empirical research are considered in order to outline a long-term framework for teacher development, one that acknowledges and encourages teacher improvisation as a higher order professional skill.

The improvising teacher is based on assumptions about professional practice that acknowledges the importance of teacher autonomy. This is articulated in a view of professionalism that is expressed by the notion of the 'authorised teacher' and defined by three concepts: authenticity, authorisation and authoring.

The final chapter of the book considers the global impact that the COVID-19 pandemic has had on education and the ways in which teachers have been at the forefront of coping and responding to the challenges caused by lockdown restrictions. This global emergency has challenged all teachers and educational leaders to draw upon their improvisatory skills, often having to make professional judgements within a policy vacuum and inadequate or non-existent government guidelines. As these restrictions have been relaxed teachers have been at the fore of creating new conditions in which learning can take place. This chapter includes examples of the improvisations that teachers have been engaged in as they have adapted to these unforeseen and unprecedented circumstances. The issues they have dealt with include developing new strategies in the ways in which information technology can be used to support learning and tackling the inequalities that have emerged regarding the communities in which they work.

This chapter provides an important reminder that the skills and values that are embodied in the improvising teacher are essential to the ways in which teachers are able to adapt and generate new practices that can support their students at times of radical social, cultural, political and global change. One of the most important lessons gained from our experience of social isolation is the importance of face-to-face encounters. This reinforces the significance of teaching as a relational and interactive activity and that the direct interaction between teacher and student is crucially important, in whatever form it takes. The improvising teacher, skilled in connecting, adapting and building relationships, is even more necessary at a time when the value of direct agential contact between teachers and students is being recognised. Across the world the way teachers and students engage in education is under review and subject to change. In whatever ways this may change we are acknowledging the importance of the seeing teaching as an improvisatory profession and the need for the professional intimacy achieved through the things that improvising teachers do best: build relationships, create dialogue and value students as individuals.

PART I
Theoretical and conceptual foundations

2 Understanding improvisation

A working definition and philosophical assumptions

Introduction

The key assumption behind this book is that teaching is fundamentally an improvisational practice. On one level this may seem a bold claim to make, yet on another level it is unsurprising and little more than a self-evident truth. As Rose points out 'improvisation is a pervasive aspect of being human, in every sphere of life, enabling existence; life without the improvisational response is difficult to imagine' (2017: 5). Given the pervasive nature of improvisation it is surprising that, until relatively recently, little attention has been given to the improvisational nature of teaching. There are a number of reasons for this. The language and practice of improvisation does not appear to fit comfortably with discourses of performativity and accountability in an educational world in which there is a global shift towards standardised curricula and pedagogy: improvisation is difficult to evaluate, assess and quantify. Furthermore, the proliferation of contexts in which improvisation takes place makes it confusing to know what is being talked about; it is a widely practised activity within the production of artistic performances and artefacts, yet it is also a feature of everyday life. Potentially all practices and social encounters contain improvisational elements. As George Lewis points out: 'improvisation is everywhere but it is very hard to see, because this ubiquitous practice of everyday life, fundamental to the existence and survival of every human formation, is as close to universal as contemporary critical method could responsibly entertain' (2013). Therefore it is unsurprising to find that there are a multiplicity of senses and significances of the word and that they are not necessarily compatible with each other (Durant, 1984). However, the move towards trans-disciplinary practice and research in the emerging field of critical studies in improvisation is a significant development in which 'the humanistic and scientific study of improvisation can provide us with new understandings of the human condition' (Lewis, 2013). Given that this book is concerned with making important claims about the importance of the improvising teacher, it is important to establish at the outset what is meant when talking about improvisation.

DOI: 10.4324/9781003223207-3

Approaches to definition

There are three positions that can be taken when attempting to tackle the issue of understanding and defining improvisation. The first is a dualistic approach in which improvisation is defined in relation to something else, usually composition. Dualisms, as Seidman (1994) points out, are based on linguistic and social hierarchies in which one concept is seen in terms of what it is not and in which the two terms are seen as unequal. In the case of the composition/improvisation binary, composition is presented as the superior form of creativity in cultural terms, deemed to have greater cultural value on the basis that it is 'thought through', that rational thinking has taken place to redraft and refine the composers' intentions. In comparison to this an improvisation appears to be made up 'on the spur of the moment', a view that does not take into account the time and effort the improviser may have put in to preparing for the improvisation. A dualistic approach consequently misrepresents not only the reality but also the value of many improvisational acts.

A second approach to definition recognises that 'linguistically organised subjective and social orders are never fixed or stable; meanings are always unstable, shifting, multi-vocal, and sites of contestation' (Seidman, 1994: 19). This approach to defining improvisation is found in a seminal paper by Alan Durant, *Improvisation – Arguments after the fact* (1984):

> The word 'improvisation', as the central term defining an area of musical activity, contains a surprisingly wide range of senses and significances. Not all of these are necessarily compatible with each other, and so it is helpful to begin to chart them, since particular senses in play can shift and change while playing or listening to improvised music, as well as in the more abstract considerations of it. It is even possible to argue that this variety in the senses of 'improvisation' has contributed, over a long period, to the confusion which obscures and complicates both the practice and the surrounding theory of this area of contemporary music making.
>
> (Durant, 1984: 5)

The variety of senses noted by Durant suggest that it may be impossible to arrive at an 'exact' definition of improvisation. Indeed there may well be no need for this as it can be argued that most people are aware when they are improvising or experiencing an improvised action or object.

A third position regards engaging in issues of definition as an inessential, a limiting and pointless activity. As the writer Toni Morrison pertinently observes, 'definitions belong to the definers, not the defined' (Grice et al., 2001: 9) a position also taken by Fischlin and Heble (2004). Their view of improvisation is as an always contingent and potentially non-monologic form of expression, which suggests that human agency cannot be contained by form. They resist defining improvisation (and the related concept of community) on the grounds that:

> ... to do so would be to limit the kinds of potential that both invite. Both (improvisation and community) exceed definition because they are polymorphous and polysemic. Both are contradictory to expectations of form even as both are most defined by their capacity to reinvent or to comment on already established forms ... As a fundamental site for the confrontation with choices made in a social order, improvisation cannot but engage, animate, and critique the social contexts it speaks to. There are no limits to what an improvisation can or cannot be. (31)

This study argues against claims that improvisation is indescribable or un-definable, taking a stance that asserts 'both the possibility and usefulness of an academic and theoretically refined consideration of improvisation' (Landgraf, 2014: 3). Indeed such an undertaking is a necessity in order to present an academically robust case for the concept of the improvising teacher. Whilst accepting Fischlin and Heble's argument that definition limits the kind of potential it invites (and acknowledging the slipperiness and incompleteness of any individual definition), there is an argument for 'charting' (in Durant's words) the range of contexts and meanings attributed to improvisation in order to inform our understanding of this multi-faceted and varied field of study.

What follows is a genealogical approach given that 'improvisation cannot be viewed independently of the social and cultural context of its articulation' (Landgraf, 2014: 11). This methodology aims to uncover how improvisation has been understood in different cultural contexts in order to enrich our understanding of the possibilities for improvisational practice within teaching, a methodology informed by Williams's 'Keywords' (1983). However, engaging with the historical derivation of words and meanings should not be confused with identifying a 'proper meaning' or a foundational definition. Williams calls this a 'sacral attitude' to words where the Classical roots hold the true meaning and that subsequent contemporary usage is vulgar based on misunderstanding and misuse; his view is that 'The original view of words are always interesting. But what is often most interesting is their subsequent variation' (1983: 21). The examples chosen below, whilst not comprehensive, present a partial and contingent mapping of meanings, offering a foundation that invites others to extend and develop. This overview leads to a synoptic working definition of improvisation that provides a necessary conceptual framework in which to frame this study, identifying 11 characteristics that are found in improvisational activity.

Classical references

The earliest texts that mention improvisation from Western European culture come from the Ancient Greeks within the context of poetry and rhetoric. However Heraclitus, whilst not going so far as saying that life is improvisatory, comments on the fluidity of lived experience when he states that 'you never step in to the same river twice' (Barnes, 2001: 69).

Ancient Greece: Aristotle

Aristotle in 'The Art of Poetry' makes one of the first references to improvisation in relation to the origins and development of poetry.

> The instinct for imitation, then, is natural to us, as is also a feeling for music and for rhythm – and metres are obviously detached sections of rhythms. Starting from these natural aptitudes, and by a series of for the most part gradual improvements on their first efforts, men eventually created poetry from their improvisations.
>
> (Aristotle in Dorsch, 1965: 35)

Aristotle's view of improvisation is as an expression of natural aptitudes, rooted in music and rhythm leading towards an end product, 'both tragedy and comedy had their first beginnings in improvisation. … Little by little tragedy advanced, each new element being developed as it came into use, until after many changes it attained its natural form and came to a standstill' (36). Improvisation is thus perceived as a formative activity, part of the creative process, associated with artistic expression but not seen as a form of expression in its own right. Through improvisation initial ideas are generated which are then subjected to later revision and refinement.

Ancient Rome: Quintilian

Classical theories of rhetoric also acknowledge the importance of knowing how to improvise. The Roman rhetorician Quintilian (c 35–c 100 AD), viewing improvisation from a professional perspective as a practising advocate in the law courts, states

> … the crown of all our study and the highest reward of our long labours is the power of improvisation. The man who fails to acquire this had better, in my opinion, abandon the power of advocacy and devote his powers of writing to other branches of literature.
>
> (Quintilian, 1922: 133)

Quintilian distinguishes between two different kinds of improvisation: the *artless* and the *artful*. *Artless* improvisers rely solely on their ingenuity, they may have a natural talent for oral performance, but they do not spend time on their studies, they don't make scripts or plan a structure for their scripts. The *artful* improviser, however, will be skilled in the subject they are speaking about in addition to having a natural talent and being educated in the art of speaking. They will be knowledgeable in their subject and of the linguistic means that they could use. An important part of the theory of rhetoric is the acquisition of a repertoire (copia).

For Quintilian preparation is all-important, the orator should be able to speak freely, with or without notes, and that a lack of general preparation will inhibit the ability to improvise. He also outlines the different situations where improvisation is required: mishaps; when examining a witness in a trial, when it is impossible to foresee how the witness will answer; happy incidents, moments within a prepared speech when the speaker suddenly gets new insights. These classical views of improvisation outline a number of tropes that are developed in subsequent uses of the word: a natural aptitude, a creative process leading to a refined end product, a response to a mishap, a dialogic response and an insight gained 'in the moment' when delivering a prepared text and the importance of having a structure or plan to improvise on.

The Enlightenment and Romanticism

The word 'improvisation' did not enter the English language until relatively modern times; the earliest record of its usage was in 1786 when it was concerned with the extemporisation of music and verse, including the extensive elaboration of poetry or ballads. Accompanying this definition is a wider application of the word as 'the production or execution of anything offhand, any work or structure produced on the spur of the moment' (Oxford English Dictionary).

The English word 'improvisation' is derived from the Latin past participle 'improvisus' which is related to the verb 'providere': to foresee. 'Improvisus' carries connotations of the unforeseen: events or actions that are unexpected, and the Latin noun 'improvisum' would include the idea of an emergency. These connotations provide a significant shift in meaning, introducing negative associations to the idea of an improvisation. Contrasting 'improvisus' with 'providere' suggests that improvisation is about not taking care, a lack of perception or attention, of not planning ahead or having foresight.

These meanings followed the word when it passed into Italian, 'improvvisare', and French, where it produced the word 'improviser' which means 'to act without foresight or planning'. This was applied within the context of spontaneous artistic creation: 'to utter or compose extemporare'. There was also the notion of doing something hastily without the necessary preparation. In modern Italian, for example, 'improvviso' means 'unexpected, unforeseen, suddenly'.

The Enlightenment, with its emphasis on reason, scientific principles and individual genius, acknowledged improvisation as artistic practice (Mozart and Beethoven, for example, were both noted for their improvisational skills)

20 *Theoretical and conceptual foundations*

yet deemed it to be inferior to composition. In the theatre improvisational traditions such as the commedia delle' arte was considered to be 'low art' as oral traditions were increasingly marginalised and replaced by conventions that rely on the 'high art' practice of writing (Landgraf, 2014: 42).

Modernism: Kandinsky

The concept of improvisation underwent a considerable transformation during the cultural movement of Modernism. Whilst the ascription of dates to cultural movements is bound to be arbitrary, nevertheless the two decades from 1910 to 1930 'constitute an intelligible unity' (Faulkner, 1977: 13). Modernism was 'part of the historical process by which the arts have disassociated themselves from nineteenth century assumptions' (1) and involved the embracing of new sensibilities, experimentation and the discovery of new means of artistic expression.

Evidence of the new approaches to artistic expression is seen in the increasing self-consciousness that artists had concerning the creative process, with self-referentiality, or reflexivity, often being combined with high aesthetic or moral seriousness (Macey, 2000: 259). This increase in self-awareness produced a body of theoretical works to validate and explain particular forms of expression.

Modernism was especially influenced by recent scientific developments, particularly Freud and Jung's work relating to the power and significance of the unconscious mind. Emphasis was placed on individuality and subjectivity, especially regarding the unique experience of consciousness by the artist. For modernist writers this led to an interest in 'moments of epiphany', an idea introduced by James Joyce in his novel Stephen Hero (1944). The eponymous central character, passing through Eccles Street, overhears a trivial exchange between a young couple. 'This triviality made him think of collecting many such moments together in a book of epiphanies. By epiphany he meant a sudden spiritual manifestation' (188). An acknowledgement of the unconscious, the intensity of the epiphanic moment and its associated spiritual dimension all inform the significance Modernism accorded to improvisation.

The proliferation of artistic movements and their related manifestos at the start of the 20th century demonstrates a preoccupation with theories and ideas that often preceded, conditioned and predefined the nature of the art object. Gradually theorising in itself became one of the chief constituents of artistic activity and this included the first attempt to theorise improvisation. Interestingly it was in visual arts, not the performing arts, that improvisation was identified as a particular and distinct form of expression.

Kandinsky, in his treatise 'Concerning the Spiritual in Art', first published in 1911, recognised three sources of inspiration. He described them as follows:

1. A direct impression of outward nature. This I call an *Impression*.
2. A largely unconscious, spontaneous expression of inner character, of non-material (i.e. spiritual) nature. This I call an *Improvisation*.

3. An expression of a slowly formed inner feeling, worked over repeatedly and almost pedantically. This I call a *Composition*. In this reason, consciousness, purpose plays an overwhelming part. But of the calculation nothing appears, only the feeling. (Kandinsky: 1977: 57)

Kandinsky's definition is significant for a number of reasons. First, he recognises improvisation as a permissible form of expression with clearly identifiable and unique qualities. This is distinct from Aristotle's view of improvisation, which Kandinsky incorporates into his view of a composition. For Kandinsky the initial improvised outpouring was in itself an artistic product – a celebration of the moment of creation.

Second, by distinguishing between improvisation and composition he recognises that they have different, but equally valuable, qualities that celebrate different cognitive processes. The former relies on fluid intuitive thinking, the latter on the more logical and reasoned forms of thinking that promote redrafting and revision. It is at this point that we can see a divergence away from Enlightenment thinking that values reason towards a Modernist perspective that acknowledges the importance of intuition.

Third, Kandinsky emphasises the importance of 'inner character' to improvisation. Whilst some people might view spontaneous creativity as only capable of conveying superficial ideas, Kandinsky saw the opposite. Improvising, by tapping into the intuitive and unconscious elements of the mind, was an expression of spiritual nature. An improvisation, therefore, was an expression of the most powerful and profound insights and experiences that a being can have. This redressed the view that had predominated Western European art in the previous 200 years, that improvisation was an inferior form of creativity.

Late-modernism

Following the end of the Second World War a further, and distinct, phase of modernism began marked by a geographical and cultural shift. In music the centre for this movement was Paris (Griffiths, 1995: 3); in the visual arts there was a shift in art world domination from Paris to New York (Hopkins, 2000: 37). This shift also brought about new understandings and significances being attached to improvisation as a form of performativity. Examples include the act of painting, especially as seen in the approach developed by Jackson Pollock, contemporary composers turned their attention from composition towards improvisation and the practices of the Beat writers embraced spontaneous writing and the public declamation of poetry (Warner, 2013).

From the mid-60s onwards many composers and performers, encouraged by the attention given to the development of instrumental virtuosity and reacting to the restrictions of serialism, saw improvisation as an expression of musical freedom. Some musicians made an explicit link with socialism seeing improvisation as an artistic expression of political freedom

(Griffiths, 1995: 204). This was particularly evident with the musicians who supported the civil rights issues in the United States and the demonstrations and unrest that occurred in 1968. Amiri Baraka, writing as Leroi Jones about the black avant-garde musicians associated with the 'New Thing', states 'This recent music *is* significant of more "radical" changes and re-evaluations of social and emotional attitudes towards the general environment' (Jones, 1963: 235).

The mid-60s also saw the emergence in Britain, Western Europe and the United States of

> a school of completely free, collective improvisation or spontaneous music – quite distinctive .... Within these developments there has been a widespread concern with improvising without reference to any framing backcloth of 'prescriptions' or conventions.
>
> (Durant, 1984: 6)

The act of improvising took precedence over what was improvised: product became subservient to process. Instead of musical improvisations being derived from existing musical structures (for example the repertoire of jazz standards) musicians 'just played'; improvisation became the music. Whilst the spiritual aspect of improvisation had not completely disappeared (for example John Coltrane's sequence of albums; 'A Love Supreme', 'Ascension' and 'Meditations'), the social and democratic relationships established within improvised music making became regarded as a model for a democratic community and social practice (Fischlin et al, 2013).

Structuralism: Generative processes and the bricoleur

Structuralism has influenced much recent thinking and understanding of improvisation in two particularly significant fields: linguistics (Chomsky's theories of 'generative grammar') and anthropology (Levi-Strauss's concept of 'the bricoleur').

Language, as the principal tool for social interaction and grammar, is a body of knowledge shared by all language users. Chomsky's claim is that our knowledge of grammar is not only innate but is also generative: a finite number of rules for producing grammatical sentences operating on a finite vocabulary can generate an infinite number of novel sentences. This suggests that we are all capable of improvising through the medium of language and 'generative grammar'. Chomsky's theories also point to the idea that improvising is not just 'doing what you like' but that it involves a dynamic interplay between fixed (finite) elements and an individual's operation of those restrictions. Whilst Chomsky's theory has not gained traction within linguistics, it makes the important point that improvisation is dependent on structure. Far from inhibiting improvisational practice, structures and rules are enablers of generative and novel outcomes.

As Quintilian points out, one of the situations where improvisation is required is dealing with mishaps. One of the earliest associations made with the word 'improvisation' is the sense of the unforeseen, responding to an emergency situation. This is perhaps particularly evident in everyday, as opposed to artistic, contexts when improvisation is a necessary response to mishaps, mistakes and making do. This sense of improvisation as a 'making do' was appropriated by Levi-Strauss and developed into the concept of 'bricolage', the bricoleur being a person who works with their hands but uses devious means compared to a craftsman. The 'bricoleur' is adept at performing a large number of diverse tasks but, unlike the engineer, he does not sub-ordinate each of them to the availability of raw materials and tools conceived and procured for the purpose of the project. His universe of instruments is closed and the rules of his game are always to make do with 'whatever is at hand' (Levi-Strauss, 1966, 17).

Bricolage, as a process of creating something, is not concerned with the calculated choice of the right materials that are most suited for a predetermined purpose, but it involves a 'dialogue with the materials and means of execution' (Chandler, 1994). Consequently 'the bricoleur "speaks" not only with things but through the medium of things' (Chandler, 1994). This can extend beyond the pragmatic, everyday world to the realm of ideas. Levi-Strauss considered myth to be an intellectual form of bricolage in that a limited level of understanding and knowledge is applied to explain a particular phenomenon. Myths provide the gap between the known and the unknown. The idea of 'speaking through the medium of things' connects with Heidegger's view of technology (1977), which unites two definitions: a means to an end and a human activity.

Bricolage as a concept has found a wide range of applications in many fields: within the arts, cultural studies, philosophy, business, Information Technology. Of particular interest for this study is the way that bricolage has impacted upon education. Papert's constructivist theories of learning identify two styles of problem solving: the analytical and bricolage. The latter is an approach to learning and problem solving that involves experimentation, testing and playing around. This improvisatory mode of learning is acknowledged by Claxton who sees learning as 'knowing what to do when you don't know what to do' (Claxton, 1999: 3).

Post-modern/ecological perspectives

All areas of the cultural and intellectual scene, since the 1980s, have engaged in debates over the existence and nature of a post-modern world. Claims for post-modernity recognize

> that in the contemporary high-tech media society, emergent processes of change and transformation are producing a new post-modern society and its advocates claim that the era of post-modernity constitutes a novel

stage of history and novel sociocultural formation that requires new concepts and theories.

(Best and Kellner, 1991: 3)

One characteristic feature of post-modern thinking is the notion that a paradigm shift (Kuhn 1962) has taken place. Post-quantum physics offers an alternative perspective to the linear cause-and-affect thinking that has dominated Western thought since the Enlightenment. There is a shift away from the focus on individuals, that has been prevalent in post-Enlightenment thinking, to a holistic and systemic worldview. A 'new' understanding of life, based on post-quantum physics and non-linear dynamics, has emerged from chaos theory, complexity theory and systems theory, integrating biological, cognitive and social dimensions (Capra, 2002, xii).

This holistic and systemic worldview is derived from ecological understandings that use the principles of organisation found in ecosystems to provide insights into a range of contexts, including social organisations, highlighting the common characteristics of spontaneous creativity, networks and relationships. Ecology theory offers the view that the world is complex, subject to continual dynamic change and where development occurs through the process of emergence. Emergence is a phenomenon that:

> takes place at critical points of instability that arise from fluctuation in the environment, amplified by feedback loops. The constant generation of novelty – 'natures creative advance', as the philosopher Alfred North Whitehead called it – is a key property of all living systems.
>
> (Capra, 2002: 102)

Key concepts that underpin ecosystems are connectedness, in that everything is related; feedback, which occurs between the interacting elements of the system and self-organisation/emergence. Self-organisation, as defined by Stacey et al. (2000), is the process by which local interaction between parts of a system produces emergent patterns of behaviour of a coherent kind in the whole, all of which takes place without an a priori grand design. The emergence of new forms of order takes place at critical points of instability.

Such eco-literate approaches use the principles of organisation found in ecosystems for creating sustainable human communities. The natural world's capacity for spontaneous self-organisation is mirrored in the improvisatory nature of the social world. From an ontological perspective this acknowledges the frequently cited pre-Socratic views of Heraclitus that the world is all flux and change, a constant state of becoming and that 'you never step into the same river twice'. Evidence of the pervasive ontology that sees the world as improvisatory can be found in the many ways in which improvisation has been used as a metaphor in order to gain an understanding into a range of social and cultural contexts. The metaphor of 'the jazz band', for example, has been used to provide insights into a range of contexts from organisation theory, leadership to the meaning of life (Sorensen, 2013).

These perspectives offer a holistic worldview in which the term 'ecological' is associated with the concept of 'deep ecology' in which there is no separation of humans from the natural environment and where the world is seen as a network of phenomena that are fundamentally interconnected and interdependent (Capra, 1996). The process of emergence is seen as the consequence of a dynamic relationship between design structures (the fixed and non-negotiable aspects of a system) and the informal generative 'emergent' structures (Capra, 1997). These assumptions are also shared by post-humanist theorists such as Braidotti (2013) who view the common denominator of the post-human condition as 'an assumption about the vital, self-organising and yet non-naturalistic structure of living matter itself' (2).

Defining improvisation: a field of meanings

This overview of the different senses clearly demonstrates how misunderstandings have arisen over the meaning of improvisation and the value that has been ascribed to it. Whilst a single definition is not possible (and may not be necessary or desirable), the way in which the concept of improvisation becomes constructed is important as it defines its role in practice and specifically within the current context of teaching. The approach taken by this study is to embrace the multiple ways of understanding improvisation and to recognise the diverse possibilities that emerge from this field of meanings. This unbounded field is open to admitting further assumptions, expectations and parameters of improvisatory practice.

By subjecting all of the above examples to an analytical coding process 11 key characteristics of improvisational practice can be identified. These are listed in Table 2.1 and each characteristic is described below.

Improvisation is an *intentional* act, not a philosophical concept. It is a specific mode of action, a particular way of doing things. Improvisation does

Table 2.1 The 11 key characteristics of improvisational practice

Improvisational practice is characterised by:

1. Intentionality
2. Requiring a context and structure
3. Being a form of creativity (either process or product)
4. Occurring spontaneously and taking place in 'real time'
5. Unpredictability
6. Being intuitive and spiritual
7. Uniqueness
8. Dialogic interaction
9. Being a type of intelligence, a mode of thinking
10. Being rooted in practice
11. Being either artful or artless

not occur accidentally, although it may constitute a response to accidents; improvisation is therefore a deliberate way of acting either through want or need. This suggests that improvisation is rule guided rather than law governed. However, there needs to be recognition that improvisation is possible before it can become part of practice. The commitment to improvise is a pre-requisite in order to develop skills and understanding as an improviser. This also raises the issue of power, of having permission to improvise, which can either be given by someone else or is a permission granted to the self. The intention to improvise contains a paradox: the intention to act without intention.

Improvisation does not exist as an activity in its own right, there is no such thing as 'pure improvisation'. Improvisation takes place within a *context*. There are three broad contexts in which improvisation exists; in addition to the social world (real-life contexts) and artistic practices, post-structuralist views suggest that the natural (non-human) world is improvisatory. The context within which an improvisation takes place will have some predetermined structural features and these generate improvisational activity. Given that improvisation is rule bound then it can be said to have meaning.

Improvisation is a form of *creativity*; a generative process can be spontaneous but need not be totally so. New material generated from the defining context can include the adaptation and/or repetition of previous material. Previously thought of ideas can be reintroduced, often with the intention of creating a sense of improvisation. The creative quality of improvisation is present in every context: functional or artistic. This acknowledges that creativity (with a small c) is present in all aspects of life. Whilst some considerations of improvisation view it as an expression of unbridled creativity, this study acknowledges that 'improvisation cannot be decoupled from structure and repetition' (Landgraf, 2014: 11). Improvisational creativity can be described as a process of emergence, the consequence of the dynamic interplay between 'fixed' non-negotiable design structures and generative structures created by informal networks and communities of practice (Capra: 2002).

Emergence, as a *spontaneous action,* takes place in 'real time'. Unsurprisingly, perhaps, those art forms that exist in real time (the performance arts of music, theatre, dance, poetry and story-telling) are most readily able to admit improvisational elements. Artistic forms that exist through objects and are not real-time dependent (for example books and paintings) can include improvised elements but most often these refer to spontaneous actions that inform the creative process. The stream of consciousness writing of Jack Kerouac and the drip paintings of Jackson Pollock are two examples. Once an improvisation comes to an end it cannot be repeated, certainly not in the same form. Recording and documentation can never capture the real essence and quality of an improvisation as this is related to the moment in time in which it takes place. It is the lived experience of what happens 'on the spur of the moment' that is essential to improvisation.

The possibility of spontaneous action means that the course of an improvisation is *unpredictable*. To improvise is to exist within a moment in time, to act without forethought, to not know what will happen until it happens. Although an improviser may have an overall plan or structure for what they are going to do, there will be decisions that will be made 'in the moment'. Being spontaneous is about deciding not to control the future. Keith Johnstone describes this as 'learning to walk backwards' which has an impact upon the way that improvised activity is structured.

> He (the improviser) sees where he has been, but pays no attention to the future. His story can take him anywhere, but he must still 'balance' it and give it shape, by remembering events that have been shelved and reincorporating them. Very often an audience will applaud when earlier material is brought back into the story.... They admire the improviser's grasp since he not only generates new material, but remembers and makes use of earlier events that the audience itself may have temporarily forgotten.
> (Johnstone, 1979: 116)

Consequently every improvisation will be *unique*. One of the requirements of an improvisation is that it should be evidently different to other acts that have taken place within similar or the same constraints. An improviser has to come up with new material. A jazz improviser would be expected to create a different solo every time she plays the same tune.

Improvisation requires spontaneous decisions. There is no time to analyse what should happen; the improviser *acts intuitively*. An intuitive act appears to be rational but is performed without the conscious adaptation of means to ends. An intuition is the immediate apprehension of an object by the mind without the intervention of the reasoning process. The validity of an intuitive act is its appropriateness. Linguists, for example, understand intuition to be a language user's knowledge of or about language, used in deciding questions of acceptability. Intuitions are the consequences of unconscious responses, which can be associated with spiritual experiences. Hence for Kandinsky the intuitive and unconscious mode of creativity is linked with spiritual expression.

Given the importance of context improvisational activity is derived from *dialogic interaction* between the improviser and the context. Interaction will take place in many ways and on different levels. The improviser will interact with the materials, the other improvisers, the audience, things that happen in the moment. The improviser has to develop a sense of being 'wide open' to influences in the moment. An important feature of improvisation is the relationships that are made, the connections that are established with other improvisers, the audience, the environment, the tradition or idiom. Above all an improvisation is concerned with the interaction between fixed elements (the designed structures) and elements that can be changed and adapted (the generative structures). As Quintilian points out there is a need for improvisation when not knowing how a witness will respond to a question.

28 *Theoretical and conceptual foundations*

The unpredictable nature of improvisation means that the improviser is continually faced with uncertainty, of not knowing what to do next. This means that within the moment they are learning from what is going on around them. The ability to do this suggests an *improvisational intelligence* that is akin to Claxton's notion of learning as 'knowing what to do when you don't know what to do'.

There are two final assumptions concerning improvisation that are connected. Quintilian makes the distinction between *artful* and *artless* improvisation. The skill of the artful improviser is *grounded in practice* and the acquisition of a repertoire (copia). This informs a view of improvisation that is not based on 'off the cuff' responses but is grounded in skill and experience, in other words the development of an expertise in improvisational practice. The relationship between improvisation and expertise is fundamental to the argument of this book and will be explored in greater detail in the next chapter, a point summed up by jazz saxophonist Lee Konitz 'That's my way of preparation – to not be prepared. And that takes a lot of preparation!' (Hamilton, 2007).

These 11 key characteristics can be brought together to provide a synoptic statement in order to provide a working definition that frames the understandings and assumptions that inform this study (see Table 2.2).

Table 2.2 A working definition of improvisation

Improvisation is a mode of intentional creative behaviour that can be present in all aspects of life. It takes place within 'real time' and involves spontaneity, intuition and dialogic interaction. Improvisations are unpredictable and unique as a consequence of the dynamic interplay between stability and change: between fixed, non-negotiable elements and informal generative processes. Located within specific contexts it can be an artless or an artful practice.

Philosophical assumptions of improvisation

The ways in which improvisation is understood is vitally important not only in terms of establishing common meanings but because it informs the way in which its role is defined in relation to the way that it is applied in practice (Rose, 2017). In this instance the concern is the way that improvisation is understood in relation to the practice of teaching. In the next section of this chapter, the 11 characteristics of improvisation and the synoptic working definition are used to articulate the philosophical assumptions that inform the research and underpin the concept of the improvising teacher. These assumptions are then related to three theoretical positions that provide the conceptual framework for this book.

The axiological assumption informing this study is that improvisation is a significant and socially valuable phenomenon that is relevant to the practice of teaching and has the potential to bring new insights to advanced professional practice. This assumption informs the philosophical, theoretical and conceptual frameworks that are drawn on in this book.

The ontological position acknowledges a paradigm shift (Kuhn, 1962) that has occurred over the past 30 years, characterised by an ecological sensibility. This shift in the way the world is viewed breaks with Newtonian mechanistic perspectives of cause and effect, determinism and linear predictability, replacing them with organic, non-linear and holistic approaches. This is a world of complexity, constant change and dynamic interaction that focuses on ecosystems and networks. Ecological views hold that spontaneous adaptive systems and the processes of emergence within the natural world are mirrored in the social world of humans. Emergence is the creative process found within the natural world as well as the social world, the difference being that the human capacity for conceptual thought and reflective consciousness allows for intentionality and the creation of meaning. Within social organisations emergence occurs through the dynamic interplay between designed structures (those created for a purpose, embodying meaning and containing the non-negotiable formal structures of an organisation) and the emergent structures (created by informal networks and communities of practice) (Capra, 2002).

The ontological assumption therefore is that the natural world is continually changing and, given that non-human nature does not have intention, can be called quasi-improvisatory given its capacity for self-organisation that reflects the Heraclitian view that 'you never step into the same river twice' (Barnes, 1987: 69). On the other hand, the social world, constructed in part through the human capacity for cognition, intentional action and self-awareness, can be described as improvisational.

The dialogic and relational characteristics of improvisation inform the ways in which knowledge is generated, arising from interactions and negotiations. These epistemological assumptions are congruent with theories of social constructionism (Burr, 2003; Gergen, 2009) that view knowledge as being personal, subjective and unique and that, through reflection, it is possible to 'know thyself'. A distinction has to be made between social constructionism and constructivist theories in which the latter claim that knowledge lies in the minds of individuals who construct *individual* meaning on the basis of their experience and where social constructionism is concerned with the idea that individuals construct *social* meaning through their shared realities and their social interaction. Whilst there is no single feature that defines a social constructionist position, the foundations of this theory are based on one or more of the following assumptions: a critical stance is taken towards taken-for-granted knowledge, all ways of understanding are historically and culturally relative, knowledge is sustained by social processes and people construct knowledge between them and knowledge and social actions go together (Burr, 2003). This latter point is of particular significance considering that improvisation is very much concerned with creative actions that take place in the moment. Shotter's reformulation of social constructionism is relevant in that it goes beyond language to acknowledge the importance of 'our spontaneous bodily reactions to events occurring around us' (2008: iii) and to focus 'on spontaneously expressed, unique, bodily activities, on unique events' (iv). This marks an important shift from the cognitive to the perceptual, where the focus is on our spontaneously responsive, living bodily activity and where this activity is expressive to others. Shotter brings attention to 'events that 'just happen to us' rather than on those of our activities we perform deliberately and self-consciously' (viii).

Further theoretical understanding of improvisation is provided by critical theory, specifically the epistemological claims of Habermas, whose theory of knowing 'impels the kind of reasoned and compassionate reflection and self-reflexivity that results in benevolent action' (Lovat, 2013: 70). Habermas argues that self-reflection produces an authentic learning that is beyond the *techne* if the goal of learning is to be one befitting being human. By acknowledging the subjective nature of knowing in which 'facts are never given in isolation from the minds that received them' (Ferre, 1982: 761), Habermas shows an interest in the way that the mind works in constructing reality especially in relation to what he called the 'critical/self-reflective' form of knowing. This form of knowing has an emancipatory intent in which our autonomy as a knower will make us reflect critically on our subject matter, our sources and ultimately ourselves as agents of knowing.

This theory of knowing informs Habermas's theory of communicative action, a theory that connects the profound knowledge gained from self-reflection with action, making a stand for social justice. The concept that lies at the heart of this theory is that of the *lifeworld* (where communicative action takes place). This is distinguished from the oppositional world of the *system* (defined by power and money and where strategic action takes place).

The *lifeworld* is where subjects arrive at common and mutual understanding that facilitates shared action based on recognising the mutual compatibility of the validity claims that are being put forward. It is a concept for the everyday world that we share with others, the informal and unmarketised domains of social life which include family, household, culture and so forth; 'these unregulated spheres of sociality provide a repository of shared meanings and understanding, and a social horizon for the everyday encounters with other people' (Finlayson, 2005: 51–52). The shared meanings and understandings of the lifeworld provide a unity, but not a totality, that is open to change.

The lifeworld has three functions:

1. It provides a context for action – a stock of shared assumptions and background knowledge, of shared reasons on the basis of which agents may reach consensus. It is a force for social integration.
2. Overall the lifeworld is conservative of social meaning, in that it minimises the risk of dissent, disagreement, and misunderstandings that attends any individual instances of communication and discourse.

3. It is the medium of the symbolic and cultural reproduction of society, the vehicle through which traditions are passed on. Under normal conditions, that is in the absence of massive social upheaval, the lifeworld serves as the medium for the transmission and improvement of all kinds of knowledge: technical, practical, scientific and moral.

The contrasting relationship between the lifeworld and the system mirrors the relationship between the two structures that create the conditions for emergence: the system relating to the design structures and the lifeworld with the emergent structures. It is this relationship that makes the theory of communicative action particularly important when attempting to understand the improvisational nature of social interaction in teaching. Critical/self-reflective knowing is impelled by the cognitive interest in being free to think one's thoughts and so to engage in *praxis*. This mode of knowing of necessity acknowledges the knowledge of the learner as well as the teacher. This has the potential to create a symmetrical relationship between teacher and learner in which there is a more equal distribution of power, where the teacher delegates power to the learner so that they have the confidence to be in control of their own learning. This can lead to a role-reversal where the teacher becomes the learner and the learner becomes the teacher. The challenge of this position is that the extent of the learners knowing may extend beyond the teacher. The type of learning proffered by critical/self-reflective knowing can be described in terms of equity and social justice:

> The norm is a distortion-free model of a communication situation ... (where) there exists no repressive dominance, no asymmetry or inequality among the participants of the educational process.
> (Van Manen, 1977: 227)

Habermas's theories of knowing and communicative action offer valuable tools for analysing improvisational practice that is based on interaction, dialogue, relational action and reaction and providing epistemological explanations for:

- distinguishing between instrumentalist approaches to education and more holistic and values based approaches;
- authentic pedagogies centred on emotional values;
- the centrality of the relationship between teacher and student within educational discourse;
- an improvisational view of teacher expertise that privileges self-reflective practice and relational pedagogies;
- a critique of neoliberal education policies and the reconceptualisation of the continuing professional development of teachers;

32 *Theoretical and conceptual foundations*

- the nature of power relationships between teachers and students as well as power relationships between teachers, other school staff, school leaders and parents;
- having the power (or permission) *to* improvise as well as the power *of* improvising.

One issue that is particularly pertinent to understanding improvisation is the issue of teleology, the branch of philosophy that deals with final causes or end states, asking why a particular phenomenon becomes what it becomes. Improvisations, as real-time spontaneous creative activities, are interactive, unique but also unpredictable. Improvisations offer an unknowable end state; there is never any certainty what will happen in an improvisation or where and when it will come to an end. From an organisational perspective this can be problematical as it runs counter to notions of cause and effect. As has been seen complexity theory offers a worldview that is organic, non-linear and holistic, and it is within the strand of complexity sciences known as complex adaptive systems that this issue is addressed.

The theory of complex adaptive systems (Stacey et al., 2000) uses an agent-based approach and is concerned with formulating rules of interaction for the individual entities making up a population or system. Complex adaptive systems involve a large number of agents who each behave according to principles of local interaction. No individual agent or group of agents determine the pattern of behaviour that the system as a whole displays, or how patterns evolve and neither does anything outside the system. The simulation of complex adaptive systems is flocking, and emergence is seen as the consequence of local interaction between agents; such unpredictable end states are called Transformative Teleologies.

The central proposition in Transformative Teleology (Stacey et al., 2000) is that human actions and interactions are processes, not systems, and the coherent patterning of these processes becomes what it becomes because of an intrinsic capacity for interaction and relationship to form coherence. The emergent form is radically unpredictable, but it emerges in a controlled or patterned way because of the characteristics of the relationship itself, to do with conflicting constraints and the self-controlled dynamics of creation and destruction in conditions at the edge of chaos. Organisations, instead of being seen as systems, are viewed as highly complex processes of people relating to each other, referred to as Complex Responsive Processes.

The three theoretical perspectives of social constructionism, critical theory and transformative teleology have been selected due to their shared commonalities and distinct differences in order to provide an ontological, epistemological and teleological framework in which to critically and conceptually engage with and understand improvisation within the context of teaching. The commonalities of these theories are summarised in Table 2.3.

Table 2.3 Commonalities between social constructionism, critical theory and transformative teleology

Social Constructionism	Critical Theory	Transformative Teleology
World is characterised by change, flux, emergence and process		
Critical stance towards taken-for-granted knowledge	A movement towards emancipatory action that is based on critical/self-reflective knowing	A movement towards a future that is under permanent construction by the moment itself. No mature or final state
Ways of understanding are historically and culturally relative		
Focus away from individual to interaction	Acknowledges the centrality of relationships	A focus on relationships as Complex Responsive Processes
Knowledge sustained by social processes and people constructing knowledge between them	The lifeworld seen as context for action based on shared meaning and assumptions	Perpetual iteration of identity and difference, continuity and transformation
Knowledge and social actions go together: need to focus on dialogism (language) and action (spontaneous, bodily responsiveness and interactions)	Normative agenda concerned with education as a human values based enterprise directed towards democracy and social justice	
Anti-essentialist		
	Explicit acknowledgement of issues relating to power and powerlessness	Implicit acknowledgement of power

Chapter summary

Starting from the assumption that improvisation is a complex concept to understand given the wide range of meanings that are attributed to it, this chapter has provided a genealogy of the changing senses and significances of the word. This has led to the creation of a synoptic statement which functions as a working definition for the empirical study. The philosophical assumptions (axiological, ontological and epistemological) have been outlined. Three theoretical positions, congruent with the view of improvisation that has been developed, have been selected in order to provide a conceptual and critical framework for understanding improvisation in relation to the context of teaching. Teaching is viewed from an ecological perspective, situated within the multi-dimension contexts of schools that are complex adaptive systems. As a relational practice teaching requires the capacity for continual adaptation and personalisation. This requires the creating of conditions 'in which teachers' individual characteristics and belief systems are acknowledged as crucial to how they interact with factors within the environment' (Daly et al., 2020: 654).

3 Understanding expertise and the lexicon of advanced professional practice in teaching

The lexicon of advanced professional practice

One of the key objectives of this book is to provide a greater understanding of 'great' or 'effective' teaching. This is sometimes referred to as 'best practice', 'excellent', or 'outstanding' teaching, but a preferential term, used here, is advanced professional practice. The quality of teaching has long been understood as the main variable regarding variation in student outcomes (Barber and Mourshed, 2007). Consequently improving the effectiveness of teachers has become a common global goal of education systems with education reforms spreading across the world like 'a policy epidemic' (Levin, 1998). This process, driven by a rhetoric of 'standards' and 'accountability', has given rise to a performativity agenda characterised by three strands of policy and practice: an audit and target-based culture, an interventionist regulatory mechanism and a market environment (Wilkins, 2011). Ball (2003) describes performativity as a technology, a culture and a mode of regulation. It employs judgements, comparisons and displays as a means of incentive and control whilst change is based on rewards and sanctions. Critics of this system argue that performativity has led to a target chasing culture where the ends justify the means and where teachers become averse to risk. The view that 'best' practice can be transferred from one site to another prevails over notions of context-specific practice emerging through professional dialogue (Seddon, 1997). Inauthentic practice and relationships and the displacement of individual qualities are the consequences of the requirement 'to produce measurable and "improving" outputs, what is important is *what works*' (Ball, 2003: 222).

The language of the performativity agenda used to describe advanced professional practice is inconsistent and confusing, raising questions about what are the best words to use when wanting to address the issue of teacher quality. Coffield and Edwards (2009) critique the lexicon on advanced professional practice and note the interchangeable and inconsistent use of 'good', 'best' and 'effective' as descriptors of practice in official texts concerning the UK government's strategy for post-16 education; however, the same arguments can be about other phases of education. 'Best' implies that there is only one approach whilst 'good' implies that there are many approaches. Other words that are employed frequently when describing advanced professional practice are 'effective', 'excellent' and 'outstanding'. All of these terms, emerging from the performativity agenda, have accrued specific meanings determined by policy-driven criteria. An example is the way in which 'outstanding' has been defined as the highest level of judgement for teaching quality by Ofsted, the regulatory body for the inspection of schools in England.

Given that the discussion about the nature of advanced professional practice has been dominated by the principles of performativity, it is hardly surprising that views of what constitutes 'good' teaching have become an ideological issue. Seen through a political lens, directly linked to policy initiatives, the professional development of teachers has been driven by compliance and regulation. Coffield and Edwards (2009) challenge this perspective and offer an alternative for professional development based around four points:

1. That whilst currently policy determines practice there is a need for practice to determine and inform policy.
2. There is a need to acknowledge the complexities of teaching and learning and that these complexities are localised. The practice of teaching needs to be accepted as being situated and that 'good' practice cannot be decontextualised, generalised and then disseminated.
3. The paradigm of improvement adopted by policy makers in which individuals and institutions are expected to be consistently good and continually improving needs to be challenged. This linear, straight, upward progression does not fit in with psychological views of learning in which progress includes curves, plateaus and drops.
4. Attention to the primacy of the relationship between the teacher and the learner:

   The emphasis should be placed neither on learning alone, nor on teaching by itself, but on the interactive processes of teaching and learning, which should be viewed as the two inseparable sides of the same coin.
   (Coffield and Edward, 2009: 373)

Hoban (2002), looking through the lens of complexity theory, sees teaching as an art and that educational change behaves as a complex system that needs to be supported by a theoretical framework to promote long-term teacher development, a need that this book addresses. In order to avoid the limitations and consequences of perspectives informed by the performativity agenda, this book argues that views of advanced professional practice should be practice-led, acknowledged as being situated and context-specific, viewed as a journey and perceived as being relational and interactive. The shortcomings of performative and managerialist assumptions about advanced professional practice are replaced by the more theoretically and conceptually rich field of expertise and expert performance. There has been a growing interest in this field of research and the application of its findings to teaching, not least due to the fact that the process of developing expertise is potentially accessible by all teachers. It is for these reasons that theories of expertise and expert practice offer a more suitable framework for viewing advanced professional practice. Such a framework provides a sustainable and longer term perspective for approaching the professional development of teachers.

About expertise

The study of expertise as a discrete field of scientific research is a comparatively recent enterprise (Ericsson et al., 2006). Over the past 40 years research into expertise and expert performance has been undertaken within a number of discrete domains. The findings from this research, when viewed from a holistic perspective, suggest that some aspects of expertise are generalisable and that an understanding of expertise in one domain can provide insights into expertise in other domains. As Ericsson et al. point out 'there are sufficient similarities in the theoretical principles mediating the phenomena and methods for studying them that it would be possible to propose a general theory of expertise and expert performance' (2006: 9). What are the general principles and debates that influence this discourse?

The Oxford English Dictionary defines an expert as 'a person who is very knowledgeable about or skilful in a particular area', 'a reliable source of knowledge, technique or skill and who is perceived as having authority or status by public or peers' (Ericsson et al., 2006:3). The process of becoming an expert is based on the assumption that there has been a period of practice, training or some form of education. An expert is seen as the product of extensive practice and learning, which has been estimated as being around 10,000 hours (Gladwell, 2008) and is most commonly contrasted with a novice, a person who is new to or inexperienced in a job or situation. A novice is any person who is new to any field or domain and who is undergoing training in order to meet the normative requirements of being regarded as a mature and equal participant.

Further distinctions can be made between experts and specialists, laypersons and technicians. A specialist is someone who has to be able to solve a problem, whilst an expert has to know its solution. In contrast to an expert is the layperson, who might have a general understanding but not have an expert knowledge. Occupying the middle ground between expert and layperson is the technician, a worker with proficiency in a relevant skill and technique who has a relatively practical understanding of theoretical principles. The expertise that distinguishes the expert from novices, specialists, laypersons and technicians are the characteristics, skills and knowledge that allow for superior performance.

In order to understand the relationship between expert knowledge and exceptional performance, attention has been given to cognitive structures and processes. The fundamental research endeavour therefore is to describe what it is that experts know and how they use this knowledge to achieve levels of performance that most people assume requires extreme or extraordinary ability. Research is therefore governed by the attempt to understand the relationship between knowledge and achievement (Ericsson et al., 2006).

Two main academic approaches have been used to understand this relationship. The first is the psychological approach, which sees expertise as a characteristic of individuals, a consequence of the human capacity for extensive adaptation to physical and social environments. This perspective defines experts either by intrinsic individual characteristics (cognitive psychology) or by their working contexts and social interactions (social psychology). Related to this latter perspective, and pertinent to this study, is the view that expertise is an emergent property of a community of practice, and that expertise is socially constructed.

The second approach is sociological, which is concerned with the importance of professions, of specific qualifications, social status and the related issues of power, influence and agency. The roots of the sociological perspective on expertise are found in Plato's 'Noble Lie' (Plato, 1974) and historically the debate concerning experts and expertise begins here. In answer to the question as to which of the governors should govern and who should be governed, Plato suggests that the best skilled (the experts) should do this; 'we must pick the ones who have the greatest skills in watching over the community' (Plato, 1974: 178). The governors would need to show they place the interests of the community over their own self-interest and should be selected through tasks and tests. The 'Noble Lie' would protect them by stating that their position, and those of the other tiers of society, was fashioned by the gods. Through this myth came the idea of an elite form of specialist (the Philosopher King) who held expert knowledge that was authoritative and intrinsically linked to notions of power. Nevertheless this raises the question of 'who shall guard the guardians?' What should the relationship be between experts and specialists on the one hand and leaders, generalists and democracy on the other (Collins and Evans, 2007)? The sociological view of expertise leads us to consider the associated issues of authority and agency. This point is picked up and explored further in the discussion of professionalism in Chapter 4.

The characteristics of experts are closely associated to the domain in which expertise is demonstrated. As Ericsson (2000) points out:

1. measures of general basic capacities do not predict success in a domain;
2. the superior performance of experts is often very domain specific and transfer outside of the domain is surprisingly rare;
3. systematic differences between experts and less proficient individuals nearly always reflect attributes required by experts during their lengthy training.

Chase and Simon's study of chess players (1973) suggests that expert performance is an extreme case of skill acquisition. Other research indicates that experience in itself is insufficient but that deliberate practice is essential to develop expert performance. Gladwell's notional figure of 10,000 hours, 'the magic number of greatness' (2008: 41), raises an important question concerning expertise and the nature/nurture debate. Is expertise an innate talent or can it be developed? The 10,000 hours rule suggests that expertise can be nurtured and, as such, provides a strong argument for the value of expertise and expert performance as an area of academic study. The next section provides an overview of some of the theories of expertise that are regularly cited as being important within the literature and are particularly relevant when attempting to understand expertise within the context of teaching.

Theories of expertise

Dreyfus and Dreyfus

One of the more important and influential theories of expertise is the five-stage model proposed by Dreyfus and Dreyfus (1986). This is described as a fluency theory (Winch, 2010) in that it focuses on the performance of experts and their way of working which is seen as not only being of a high quality but is conducted without hesitation, with rapidity and in such a way that they cannot fully explain what they are doing.

The theory outlines a process of skill acquisition that goes through five stages, summarised in Table 3.1.

This theory has been used within professional settings such as nursing (Benner 1984) and teaching (Goodwyn, 2011), where it helps to operationalise our understanding of teacher expertise. Goodwyn maps the five levels against the phases of teacher education and professional development in England and Wales. The novice stage relates to the process of working towards Qualified Teacher Status (QTS), with the advanced beginner stage aligned with becoming a newly qualified teacher (NQT). The competence phase is recognisable as the point that is reached after two or three years when teachers have gained experience of the longer time cycles within education: the term, the school year and the assessment and examination cycles. The understanding that is gained from this experience allows an appreciation of the longer-term goals for both the individual teacher and the school. Goodwyn sees a clear link between the proficiency stage and the notion of crossing performance-related thresholds that determine higher levels of pay and the point where teachers begin to develop their own schema (or maxims) to guide their actions.

It is worth looking in detail at the description of level 5 in order to understand how Benner has built upon the Dreyfus model in order to describe expert nursing:

> The expert performer no longer relies upon an analytic principle to connect their understanding of the situation to appropriate action. The expert

Table 3.1 Summary of Dreyfus and Dreyfus (1986) five stages of skill acquisition

Level	Description
Level 1 – Novice	A rigid adherence to taught rules or plans
	Little situational perception
	No discretionary judgement
Level 2 – Advanced beginner	Guidelines for action are based on attributes or aspects (aspects are characteristics of situations recognisable only after some prior experience)
	Situational perceptions are still limited. All attributes and aspects are treated separately and given equal importance
Level 3 – Competent	Able to cope with crowdedness
	Now sees actions at least partially in context of longer-term goals
	Conscious and deliberate planning
	Standardised and routinised procedures
Level 4 – Proficient	Sees situations holistically rather than in terms of aspects
	Sees what is most important in a situation
	Perceives deviations from the normal pattern
	Decision making less laboured
	Uses maxims for guidance, whose meaning varies according to the situation
Level 5 – Expert	No longer relies on rules, guidelines or maxims
	Intuitive grasp of situations based on deep tacit understanding
	Analytic approaches used only in novel situations or when problems occur
	Vision of what is possible

nurse, with an enormous background experience, now has an intuitive grasp of each situation and zeroes in on the precise region of the problem without wasteful consideration of a large range of unfruitful alternative diagnoses and solutions. The expert operates from a deep understanding of the total situation. Their actions are intuitive and often the justification for a particular decision will be that 'it felt right or it looked good'. The performer is no longer aware of features and rules; his/her performance becomes fluid and flexible and highly proficient. This is not to say that the expert does not use analytic tools. Highly skilled analytic ability is necessary for those situations with which the nurse has had no previous experience ... when the expert gets the wrong grasp of the situation and then finds that events and behaviours are not occurring as expected.

(Benner, 1984, cited in Goodwyn, 2011: 36)

What stands out from this description is the emphasis the Dreyfus model places on intuition and unconscious competence when performing at the highest levels. This highlights a paradox of expert performance, which is that experts are often unable to explain or articulate their expertise. Often their actions and responses to situations are automatic and intuitive, taking place at such a speed that they find it difficult later to explain and analyse exactly what they have done or why. This presents a problem when researching expertise as experts may be unable to articulate what they do and how they do it.

The view of expert performance offered by Dreyfus and Dreyfus is of fluid and flexible approaches to situations in which decisions are guided by an intuitive understanding, which is informed by extensive experience and practice. Analytical approaches are deployed when problems and new situations are encountered. Furthermore the expert is unable to give a full account of what they do.

There are a number of critical issues that have been raised regarding this theory. Eraut (1994) notes that the Dreyfus and Dreyfus model 'provides an analysis of skilled behaviour under conditions of rapid interpretation and decision making, in which the logically distinct processes of acquiring information, following routines and making decisions are fully integrated' (128). He holds with the view that the theory accounts for the greater complexity of professional work and the time required to develop expertise but sees two shortcomings in the theory. The first is that it neglects the problem of expert fallibility, and the second is that the proportion of professional work that it covers is unclear.

Winch (2010) offers a more comprehensive critique of this theory on several counts, which can be summarised as follows:

1. If many (if not all) activities require a theoretical basis for successful, let alone expert, practice then this model would not apply to them.
2. The model focuses on action (performance) and not on outcomes and, as expert performance ought to produce excellent results this is a shortcoming.
3. There is a tendency to see a correlation between action and the activity or structural functions of the brain, which are then subsequently subsumed into identities (for Winch this is the most important criticism).
4. There is a question as to whether the field of action should be the occupation or the task, Winch argues that the primary attribution should be the task.
5. The concept of excellence is seen as being problematic within the context of expert performance as an excellent action or outcome is attributed on the basis of criteria appropriate to that activity or outcome being held by the relevant community. Winch questions whether understanding action can be conceptually detached from understanding the intended outcome of the action.

Nevertheless the intuitive aspect of expert performance highlights its improvisational nature. Experts are able to make decisions 'in the moment', spontaneously responding to the situations that they face in which their actions are informed by their tacit knowledge.

Schön: the reflective practitioner

Another influential theory that shares similar assumptions that expertise is based on tacit knowledge is Schön's concept of the reflective practitioner (Schön, 1983). Schön seeks to find a more effective way to understand the intuitive and implicit thinking of a professional than that afforded by rational analysis. His search is for 'an epistemology of practice implicit in the artistic, intuitive processes by which some practitioners do bring to situations of uncertainty, instability, uniqueness and value conflict' (Schön, 1983: 49). Schön's view of professional practice is one in which the knowledge and thought of a practitioner are most evident in their actions. Therefore, the accomplished professional is one that engages in reflection. Schön makes the distinction between two kinds of reflection: *reflection in action*, which occurs during the course of professional action and *reflection on action*, which takes place after the action has been completed. Winch (2010) raises the point that in order to understand this theory you need to understand both the basis for reflection and the subject matter. Eraut (1994) finds it more helpful to see this theory as one of metacognition deployed during skilled behaviour.

However, the concept of 'the reflective practitioner' has had a significant impact on approaches to professional development and the progress towards expertise. Teaching in particular has embraced the idea of 'reflective practitioner' as being an essential, and demonstrable, aspect of professionalism. Habermas also places great import on self-reflection arguing that it produces an authentic form of learning that goes beyond the *techne* (the skill of doing something), in which our autonomy as a knower makes us reflect critically on our subject matter, our sources and ultimately ourselves as agents of knowing. Schön highlights the importance of the relationship between action and critical thinking, two distinct forms of knowledge that Ryle (1945) describes as knowing *how to* and knowing *that*.

A four-stage model of competence

A further theoretical framework that is based on assumptions of the importance of tacit knowledge is the four-stage model of competence, which is widely used in leadership training courses to assist in understanding the process of acquiring expertise. This model has been attributed to a number of authors: Dubin (1962, cited in Snowdon and Halsall, 2019), Robinson (1974), Howell (1982), without anybody being able to definitely confirm its origin.

This model is usually presented as a matrix organised along two axes: the horizontal axis being a continuum from incompetence to competence and the vertical axis being a continuum from unconscious to conscious thought. This produces four interlinked stages:

1. The *unconscious incompetence* stage: the learner has had no experience and therefore they have no comprehension of what is required to perform a task. They are not aware of what they don't know or what they cannot do.
2. The *conscious incompetence* stage: the learner attempts the activity and begins to understand how much information there is that they need to be aware of and the range of skills involved. They become aware of what they cannot do and what they need to learn and understand.
3. The *conscious competence* stage: this stage is arrived at through practice and instruction so that the learner is able to undertake these tasks but needs to give attention to each small detail.
4. The *unconscious competence* stage: this stage is only reached through continual practice and reaching a level of expertise within a particular domain. At this stage, all of the skill sets are well established and actions can be undertaken without conscious thought.

This fourth stage is in accord with Dreyfus and Dreyfus's understanding of expert performance. Many experts are unable to account for what they do, and why they do it, as their actions are driven by tacit knowledge and have become unconscious competences. One way of developing their expertise further, drawing upon Schön's practice of *reflection on action*, is to enable those unconscious competences to become conscious competences once more.

The theories that have been considered so far have viewed the acquisition of expertise as an individual enterprise, a consequence of the human capacity for extensive adaptation to physical and social environments. However, as was noted earlier, another approach is to see expertise defined by working contexts and social interactions. This latter approach views expertise as a social construction. Theories supporting this view suggest that learning to become an expert is a social activity that comes from the experience of participating in everyday life. The contribution of Lave and Wenger (1991) to our understanding of social learning is of particular importance.

Lave and Wenger: communities of practice

Lave and Wenger's (1991) model of situated learning proposes that learning takes place through a process of engagement in a community of practice. The importance of this theory to this study is that expertise can be seen as being gained through interaction with others. Lave and Wenger describe a community of practice as being formed by a group of people to engage in collective learning. This is not a new idea; the source of this practice can be traced back to the medieval guilds that were formed to protect themselves from competition (Ericsson et al., 2006; Sennett, 2008).

A community of practice takes the form of a nested structure, which means that any individual can be a member of different communities of practice. Lave and Wenger describe three crucial characteristics: a domain, a community and a practice.

A community of practice has an identity defined by a shared domain of interest. Membership implies a commitment to the domain and therefore a shared competence that distinguishes members from others. In pursuing their interest in the domain members engage in joint activities and discussions to help each other and share information. They build relationships that enable them to learn from each other. Finally members of a community of practice, as the name implies, are practitioners. They develop a shared repertoire of resources: experiences, stories, tools and ways of addressing recurring problems. In short they create a shared practice, which takes time and sustained interaction.

When learning is placed within the context of social relationships (as opposed to being the acquisition of certain types of knowledge by individuals), then it raises questions about the kinds of social engagements that provide the most effective situations for learning to occur. This moves away from concerns with cognitive processes and conceptual structures that dominate much of the research. In place of this we have a view of the learning process which involves moving from 'legitimate peripheral participation' to 'full participation' as the individual becomes more competent and more involved in the main processes and practices of the domain.

> Learners inevitably participate in communities of practitioners and ... the mastery of knowledge and skill requires newcomers to move toward full participation in the socio-cultural practices of a community. 'Legitimate peripheral participation' provides a way to speak about the relations between newcomers and old-timers, and about activities, identities, artefacts, and communities of knowledge and practice. A person's intentions to learn are engaged and the meaning of learning is configured through the process of becoming a full participant in a socio-cultural practice. This social process includes, indeed it subsumes, the learning of knowledgeable skills.
>
> (Lave and Wenger 1991: 29)

Thus, communities of practice have much to say about the development of identity and, specifically, the ways in which the identity of becoming an 'expert' is arrived at. It raises questions, for example, about the ways in which participants speak, act and improvise that makes sense to the other members of the community (questions that are picked up in the empirical research that was undertaken). Learning is viewed from a holistic perspective: 'learning as increasing participation in communities of practice concerns the whole persona acting in the world' (Lave and Wenger 1991:29). The emphasis that is placed on the situated nature of learning, located in communities of practice, means that the context in which the learning takes place has to be understood. This brings attention to issues surrounding organisational culture. This is not a straightforward matter, for example it needs to take into account issues of power, the extent, for example, that power relationships inhibit entry or participation or the kinds of practice or knowledge that are favoured over others.

The theories of expertise outlined above can offer important insights into expertise within particular areas and help us to understand the general factors that govern expertise. However, as Winch (2010) points out, there is a need to be critical of the extent to which claims can be made. He argues that claims regarding the essential nature of expertise cannot be sustained, partly due to the fluid criteria used to ascertain what counts as expertise. Consequently, it is difficult to see how a general theory of expertise can be constructed, although he does acknowledge that a contribution to the greater understanding of expertise can be made through pointing to important features that may be found in a variety of different circumstances. He argues that

> the important issue in an examination of expertise is not the attainment of a general account, applicable to all cases of expertise, but rather a greater understanding of the enormous variety of what we call 'expertise' and 'experts', together with an understanding of the different conceptual dimensions in which we talk about expertise.
>
> (Winch, 2010: 136)

Sternberg and Horvath: prototype theory

A theory that takes up the issue of variety in expertise and experts is the prototype theory proposed by Sternberg and Horvath (1995), which has been developed specifically within the context of teaching. The function of the theory is to orientate thinking through a synthetic framework that is designed to encourage debate and stimulate further research. Their views are based on three assumptions:

1. That there are no well-defined standards that all experts meet and that no non-experts meet.
2. Experts bear a family resemblance to each other and it is this resemblance that structures the category of 'expert'.
3. A convenient way of talking about this is through the concept of the prototype.

A prototype is defined as that which 'represents the central tendency of all the exemplars in the category' (Sternberg and Horvath, 1995: 9) and is derived from cognitive psychology research on natural language concepts (Rosch, 1973, 1978). Rosch argues that similarity-based concepts exhibit a graded structure wherein some category members are better exemplars of the

Table 3.2 Summary of Sternberg and Horvath (1995) expert teaching prototype

Knowledge (Quantity and Organisation)	Efficiency	Insight
Content knowledge	Automatisation	Selective encoding (selecting what is and what is not in solving problems)
Pedagogical knowledge Content specific Content non-specific	Executive control Planning Monitoring Evaluating Reinvestment of cognitive resources	Selective combination (combining information in ways that is useful for problem solving)
Practical knowledge Explicit Tacit		Selective comparison (applying information acquired in another context to solving the problem in hand)

category than others: the greater the similarity between the subject and the prototype, the greater probability that it belongs to the category.

This approach leads them to construct an expert teaching profile in which expertise is organised under three headings: knowledge, efficiency and insight, the basic ways in which experts differ from novices. The features of these three areas are summarised in Table 3.2.

Sternberg and Horvath suggest that teaching expertise can be viewed as a natural category that is structured by the similarity of expert teachers to one another and represented by a prototype, reference to which enables decisions about the expert status of a teacher to be made. This approach enables distinctions to be made between experts and experienced non-experts and makes two important points. The first is that there is diversity in the population of expert teachers, and the second is that there is an absence of individually necessary and jointly sufficient features that characterise an expert teacher. This theory refutes an essentialist approach to teacher expertise in which there is a defined set of qualities, knowledge and skills that a teacher needs to acquire in order to be deemed an expert. Instead the prototype theory suggests that expertise is displayed in a number of ways and that two equally valid members of the category of expert teachers may resemble each other much less than they resemble the prototype.

This approach is aligned with Winch's critique of theories of expertise as outlined earlier and suggests that there is little value in trying to provide a generalised picture of 'the expert teacher'. Instead a more fruitful approach is to try and understand the variety of expertise that teachers have. Instead of trying to define what or who an expert teacher is, it is more important to ask 'in what ways do teachers demonstrate expertise?' This also suggests that expertise will be displayed in different ways in different contexts and this reflects the importance of 'communities of practice'.

Chapter summary

This chapter has examined the discourses of advanced professional practice in teaching, critically analysing the vocabulary used to describe 'great' teaching and the shortcomings of notions such as 'best practice', 'excellent teachers' and 'outstanding'. Given that these terms are associated with the performativity agenda it has been argued that a better way to consider advanced professional practice is to locate it within discourses of expertise and expert practice, as this is potentially accessible by all teachers. The ways in which experts and expertise can be understood have been outlined along with the characteristics of expert performance. Key theories regularly cited as being important in the literature were explored and a view of teacher expertise is offered based on a prototype model in which experts have 'family resemblances' but are not all the same.

This chapter has reconceptualised expertise in four respects:

1. Expertise is seen as a preferential way to view the advanced professional practice of teachers and that this is a long-term process.
2. Expertise is viewed as a socially constructed practice.
3. By rejecting essentialist notions and acknowledging that there is a great variety in experts and expertise; whilst all experts are not the same they bear family resemblances.
4. Given that expert practice is an unconscious competence, characterised by 'in the moment decisions' informed by tacit knowledge then it is also significantly improvisational.

In the next chapter, attention will be given to the sociological implications of the way we understand improvisation and expertise by looking at how these concepts are addressed, or not addressed, within discourses concerning professionalism.

4 Understanding professionalism and the discourses of advanced professional practice

Introduction

The improvising teacher offers a new paradigm for the way that we understand the practice of teaching, and this leads to different perceptions of how teachers learn and the processes of educational change. This chapter explores how the concept of the improvising teacher informs a different understanding of professionalism, placing this re-conceptualisation within the context of the processes that inform a long-term framework for professional development. The two strands to the development of this argument, outlined in the previous chapters, can be summarised as follows. The first is that the best way to understand advanced professional practice is through the frame of expertise and expert performance, and the second is that expert performance is fundamentally improvisatory. A view of advanced professional practice that is based on improvisation and expertise offers a radical approach to the education and development of teachers, one that values creativity, authenticity and the authorisation to make professional judgements. Over the years, the views of what it means to be 'a professional teacher' have changed and a range of discourses have emerged. The improvising teacher offers a continuation of that process of professional re-evaluation. This chapter provides an overview of those changes, considers the relationship between effectiveness and professionalism and outlines a range of discourses that currently inform contemporary educational debates.

Understanding professionalism

Professionalism is a problematic and contested concept. Grace (2014), reflecting on the changing nature of professionalism, notes that 'The idea of a "profession" (as a "calling" and not simply a job) and of "professionalism" (as a process and way of life) had its origins in religion' (ibid.: 18). He points out that the first professions of priesthood, medicine and law invested the technical activities of the practitioners with a spiritual, moral, ethical and, on occasions, political significance. This sense of vocation is something that still informs the motivations of many to join the teaching profession.

The transformation of many organisations into professions is seen as one of the key features of the emergence of 'modern' society (Bullock et al., 1988). The process of professionalisation in this context differs from a sense of a 'calling' or way of life. This process involves the development of formal entry qualifications based on education and examinations, the establishment of regulatory bodies to admit and discipline members and some degree of state-guaranteed monopoly rights. The notion of professionalism carries with it notions of power, the right to operate with autonomy along with the need to be seen to be accountable.

The monopolistic and gatekeeping function of professions leads Eraut (1994) to view professionalism from an ideological perspective, as a process by which occupations seek to gain privilege and power in accord with that ideology, 'the problem to which the concept of professionalism is said to provide an answer is that of the social control of expertise' (ibid.: 2). Expertise is regarded as the prime source of professional power.

Professions tend to be autonomous, having a high degree of control over their own affairs. This carries with it an expectation that they have the freedom to exercise professional judgement and the power to control not only its area of expertise but also its members and their interests. Professions contribute to the stratification of society, and becoming part of the 'professional class' is an aspiration for many as they enjoy relatively secure and remunerative careers and perceive a separation from people in more routine manual jobs (Giddens 1993: 235). Most professional roles are found within those sectors of the economy where the state plays a major role: in government, health and social welfare. In fact the majority of people working in professional occupations, doctors, accountants, lawyers and teachers, for example, are employed by the state.

However, the relationship that teaching has with other professions is an interesting one. Distinctions are made between the longer established professions such as doctors, lawyers, engineers and accountants with the newer professions such as social workers and teachers. Teaching has never been fully recognised as a profession mainly because it has been unable to promote and demonstrate a distinctive expertise (Beck, 2008), and as Whitty (2008) points out, teachers have never had the right to fully exercise their autonomy, as has been the case for other professions. Consequently teaching is often described as a quasi-profession, one that does not have the same status as medicine or the law yet, nevertheless, occupies a status above other 'jobs' (Adams, 2014).

The changing nature of teacher professionalism

The complexities surrounding notions of teacher professionalism can be illustrated by looking at the ways in which the professional status of teachers has changed in England over the past 200 years. Social, historical and political influences have incrementally informed the complex, and sometimes conflicting, professional expectations that teachers now face across the world.

These changes have been classified into four distinct phases (Hargreaves and Fullan, 2000):

1. The pre-professional phase
2. The autonomous professional
3. The collegial professional
4. The fourth age – post-professional or post-modern

This framework provides a useful way to demonstrate the changing professional expectations, highlighting the knowledge required to become a teacher and the approaches used to support professional development. An additional phase has been added to Hargreaves and Fullan's model: that of the 'emerging professional' that follows on from the pre-professional phase.

The pre-professional stage

In the early 19th-century, education was broadly carried out at a local level with minimal influence from the state. Education was largely religious in character and the teacher was engaged in the rudimentary delivery of basic knowledge and skills. The spread of urbanisation impacted upon both the size and the nature of schools and teachers. No longer operating individually within an informal setting they became salaried employees. Education was based on utilitarian ideals and centred upon the transmission of facts, the approach to education characterised by Gradgrind's demand for 'facts, facts, facts' in Charles Dickens novel *Hard Times* (1854).

The principles and parameters of teaching were based around common sense, the management of discipline (reinforced by the use of corporal punishment) and the ability to secure a limited proficiency in the '3Rs' of reading, (w)riting and (a)rithmatic. The assumption was that teachers were 'born not made', therefore training to become a teacher was extremely rudimentary based on watching and copying what other teachers did, a process described as 'sitting with Nellie'. There was no provision for any kind of professional development following this basic induction. The pay of teachers was determined by the results they achieved: the number of children that passed tests that ascertained their level of knowledge determined their salary.

Two significant pieces of legislation had an impact on the work of teachers: the Revised Code of 1861 and the Education Act of 1870. The former was driven by governmental concern about levels of literacy and numeracy, displaying an apparent dissatisfaction with the profession.

The emerging professional

The 1902 Education Act (the Balfour Act) began the process of inaugurating a professional status for teachers. Building on the 1870 Education Act, the control of existing schools and the responsibility for developing secondary education was placed in the hands of newly formed Local Education Authorities (LEAs). The creation of the new tier of secondary education had an impact on the training of teachers as the traditional approaches used in the pre-professional stage were deemed to be inadequate. The intention was that graduates of the new secondary schools would provide most of the teachers who would be recruited to teach in elementary schools. The most-able secondary school students would proceed to higher education and then, perhaps, would be recruited to the middle class grammar and private schools (Hoyle and John, 1995: 24). At the start of the 20th century, a number of universities created their own 'training departments' in which graduates, after completing their degree course, could study the theory and practice of education. This significantly broadened the range of knowledge that a teacher was required to have, recognising that the practice of teaching needed to be supported by some form of theoretical understanding.

Theories of education and child development were emerging, and there was particular interest in the ideas emanating from mainland Europe. Theorists such as Pestalozzi, Montessori and Piaget made important contributions to the understanding of a child's development and child-centred education in the early years, influenced by the ideas of Rousseau who in 'Emile, or On Education' (1762) argues for the essential goodness of people.

The union movement began the process of organising teachers into a professional body and by the 1920s teachers began to gain some form of professional autonomy. Whilst they were required to meet the needs of the state they were allowed a degree of independence in the work place, which granted them opportunities to develop the curriculum and new pedagogies.

The autonomous professional

The period from the 1920s to the 1970s is often viewed as a 'golden age' of teacher professionalism. A sense of 'responsible autonomy' became the hallmark of the relationship between teachers and the state and was viewed by many, especially the teachers associations and unions, as a move towards greater professionalism. This was particularly the case from the 1960s onwards when classroom practice saw the development of a broader range of teaching methods, including the wider dissemination of child-centred approaches. This was reflected in the Plowden Report *Children and their Primary Schools* (1967) that acknowledged 'to a unique extent English teachers have the responsibility and the spur of freedom' (Plowden, 1967: 312).

However, the report was critical of the fact that graduates entering the teaching profession were not required to have a professional training, and this was perceived as having an impact on the teachers standing as professionals. The desire that all teachers should achieve Qualified Teacher Status (QTS), approved by the Department for Education and Science (DES), was fulfilled in September 1970. Following this, the James Report *Teacher Education and Training* (DES, 1972) reinforced the establishment of teaching as a graduate career, proposing a radical organisation of teacher education into three stages (or cycles). The first cycle (two years) would consist of a general higher education course, and the second cycle (two years) would be a year of professional studies followed by a year as a 'licensed teacher', replacing the existing probationary year. A teacher who completed these four years would be awarded a BA (Ed). The third cycle would consist of in-service training.

The significance of the James Report was that it widened the knowledge base that was required to become a teacher. Subject knowledge and theories of education were combined with practical knowledge gained through the experience of working in a classroom. Not only was the continuing development of teachers seen as important, there was an acknowledgement that there should be a link between initial teacher training and continuing professional development. The principle of integrating teacher education into higher education was accepted by government, and throughout the 1970s colleges of education merged with other further and higher education establishments to form colleges and institutes of higher education (Mackinnon and Statham, 1999: 28).

However, whilst it might appear that teachers were gaining greater status as professionals, there were concerted challenges to their autonomy. The freedom to develop the curriculum and initiate new pedagogies was attacked by right wing educationalists who, in a series of 'Black Papers', critically compared 'progressive' developments to traditional approaches. The progressive style of education was blamed for the wider ills of society, 'a main cause not only of student unrest in the universities but of other unwelcome tendencies or phenomena' (Galton, Simon and Croll, 1980: 41). The argument against 'progressive' educational methods was played out in the media following incidents at William Tyndale primary school in north London. In 1974 some of the staff introduced radical changes resulting in disputes between teachers and school managers and a chaotic lack of control of the school and its students. The 'William Tyndale Affair' marked a turning point in modern educational history (Davis, 2002) in that the apparent failure of progressive methods in one school prompted a more interventionist approach to teaching methods and standards by central government.

This watershed was marked by, and influenced, the speech made by British Prime Minister James Callaghan at Ruskin College Oxford on 18 October 1976. He stated that the curriculum would no longer be a 'secret garden' and that all who worked within the education system would have to acknowledge the needs of the national economic agenda. This speech initiated developments that held teachers and school leaders accountable for what they taught and how they taught it. Callaghan was however careful to stake out his own position: he was not supporting the prejudices of the Black Paper writers and neither was he denying the cooperation of teachers. 'We must carry the teaching profession with us. They have the expertise and the professional approach' (Callaghan, 1976).

The collegiate professional

The issues raised in Callaghan's 'Ruskin' speech were taken further by the Conservative government that came to power in 1979 led by Margaret Thatcher. 'Thatcherism', synonymous with the politics of the New Right, introduced neo-liberal *laissez-faire* economic policies and embraced traditional conservative values of authoritarianism and hierarchical social structures epitomised by the primacy of the nation state (Hoyle and John, 1995: 40).

Greater governmental control over education was accomplished with the 1988 Education 'Reform Act' which introduced a national curriculum, national testing of students' progress and the publication of league tables which enabled comparisons to be made within schools and LEAs. However, this act was preceded by other reforms that had a significant impact upon teaching. The report 'Better Schools' (DES, 1985a) emphasised the importance of teacher quality and led to outlining approaches for teacher appraisal. However, this raised the issue that there were no guidelines or criteria against which teacher performance could be measured. Her Majesties Inspectorate (HMI) produced a paper outlining what constitutes good performance in primary and secondary schools (DES, 1985b). This was the first time that the state had outlined the characteristics of 'good' teaching.

The impact of the National Curriculum, initially constructed around a lattice framework of subjects and cross-curricular themes, and the introduction of standardised assessment tests (SATs) placed complex demands on teachers. They were required to teach skills, knowledge and understanding that lay outside of traditional subject boundaries, and students with special educational needs were incorporated into mainstream schools. This required a professional shift away from being a teacher of subjects to being a teacher of students. The challenge of introducing these changes led to the creation of collaborative cultures in schools to facilitate a co-ordinated approach to curriculum delivery and the realisation of whole school initiatives. Five days a year were allocated to in-service training, and teachers were deemed to be responsible for engaging in professional development activities. Curriculum innovation, whole school initiatives and in-service training reinforced a view of teaching as a collective and collaborative activity in which teachers learnt from each other, sharing and developing good practice.

The fourth professional age

The shift in teacher professionalism in the fourth age is aligned with the profound transformations of 21st-century society: 'the social geography of post modernity is one where boundaries between institutions are dissolving, roles are becoming less segregated, and borders are becoming increasingly irrelevant' (Hargreaves and Fullan, 2000: 51). Furthermore the 21st century introduced the digital age where information technologies and the worldwide web radically transformed the availability, creation and the dissemination of information and knowledge. The fourth professional age is one that will be familiar to most developed countries across the world.

This had, and continues to have, a profound impact on the nature of teacher professionalism, increasing the areas of work and the agencies with which teachers are expected to engage. These changes include a shift in the focus of teaching from transmitting knowledge to facilitating learning, engaging with parents, working with a wider range of professionals (including health, social services and the police) and developing the educational potential of new technologies. Since 2010, there has been a significant decline in the influence of local authorities, and the academy schools programme has led to the creation of networks or chains of schools and the development of 'self-improving school systems'. The debate on the nature of teaching as a profession is split along two lines of argument. The first argues that teaching has undergone a process of deprofessionalisation and that teachers are merely technicians responsible for the delivery of proscribed learning content. The second maintains that teachers should have an autonomy and agency as valued professionals. This debate plays out in the discourses of professional development with the former concerned with training and the latter with developing critical professionals. These two positions represent the different ends of a spectrum. However, one of the main determinants of professional practice, introduced in the 1970s, was the notion of 'effectiveness'. The next section explores how this had an impact on views of professionalism.

Effectiveness and professionalism

Understanding what makes a school 'effective' was one of the significant features of educational reform from the 1970s onwards across the world and has been a key feature of the fourth professional age. Ron Edmonds in the United States is generally credited with initiating this movement (Hopkins et al., 1994), arguing that the internal features of individual schools can make a difference and that they outweigh the influence of home or hereditary factors. The first major study in the UK, undertaken by Rutter et al., *15,000 hours: secondary schools and their effects on children* (1979), compared the 'effectiveness' of ten secondary schools in south London on a range of student outcome measures. One of the key factors of school effectiveness is concerned with understanding the qualities of effective teaching.

However, the process of defining what constitutes effective teaching is complex and controversial. As Ko et al. (2016) argue that 'effective' is a very narrow term, what is it effective of?

> Effective teaching requires criteria for effectiveness. These criteria refer to the objectives of education in general and teaching in particular. Visions about the criteria are the result of a political and societal debate, but educational professionals, teachers and schools can also take part in it.
> (ibid.: 12)

Focussing on outcomes reflects value-driven choices and priorities for the goals of education, goals that are defined politically and ideologically either by central or local government or at school or departmental level: 'a teacher is effective if he/she can accomplish the planned goals and assigned tasks in accordance with school goals' (Campbell et al., 2004: 61).

Criticisms of the teacher effectiveness movement centre on the argument that it offers a constrained view of teaching, seeing it as the accomplishment of school set goals or current ideological educational imperatives. Furthermore notions of teacher effectiveness are accompanied by demands for consistency, requiring schools to establish 'consistent patterns of teacher practices' (Ko et al. 2016: 6). Neither is it possible to ignore the impact that high stakes accountability systems have on reducing teachers' freedom to be creative and the damage this has on their professional autonomy. The concept of effectiveness provides a limited view of professionalism, one that potentially de-professionalises the teacher to the role of a technician who is tasked with the 'delivery' of proscribed learning content. In stark contrast to this is a view of a teacher professionalism that is grounded in autonomy and expertise.

Sachs (2001) articulates these two distinctly different views of professionalism as a managerialist discourse and a democratic discourse. Dualistic approaches can offer a useful heuristic, and Sachs acknowledges the problems of using such binary oppositions. However, contemporary views of professionalism and advanced professional practice as found in the fourth professional age are more complex than this binary suggests. A broader approach needs to take into account the full range of the competing voices that are engaged in this debate. It is possible to discern five discourses of advanced professional practice that can be found in contemporary educational debates:

1. The autonomous professional discourse: the reflective practitioner
2. The 'masterliness' discourse: the Masters in Teaching and Learning
3. The managerialist discourse
4. The accountability discourse
5. The globalisation discourse

The autonomous professional discourse: the reflective practitioner

This discourse has its roots in a notion of professionalism which admits autonomy and permits a high degree of control over practice. It is a view that acknowledges the status and power of teaching as a profession (a view that is more in line with professions such as medicine and the law) where professional authority is derived from expertise and permits the freedom to exercise professional judgement.

The autonomous professional discourse admits that teachers have a role to play in advancing their professional practice and their knowledge of teaching. Ryle's (1946) distinction between two main kinds of knowledge, 'knowing that' (propositional knowledge) and 'knowing how to' (practical knowledge), is useful when understanding this discourse. As Eraut (1994) points out whilst propositional knowledge underpins and enables professional action, it is 'knowing how to' that is inherent in action and cannot be separated from it. Practical knowledge, sometimes described as 'tacit knowledge' (Polyani, 1967), is significant in recognising 'that important aspects of professional competence and expertise cannot be represented in propositional form and embedded in a publicly accessible knowledge base' (Eraut, 1994: 15).

Schön's conception of the 'reflective practitioner' offers important insights to understanding the tacit nature of professional knowledge. Based on the assumption that often people do not know what they know, Schön argues that through reflection they become able to articulate their thinking and be more explicit about their practice. He outlines three levels of consciousness: knowing-in-action, reflection-in-action and reflection-on-action. Rejecting a model of professionalism that is based on technical rationality he argues for 'an epistemology of practice implicit in the artistic, intuitive processes which some practitioners do bring to situations of uncertainty, instability, uniqueness and value conflict' (Schön, 1983: 49). Acknowledging the importance of intuition is essential for understanding professional practice that is 'characterised by complexity, is dynamic and interactive and happens in a very specific and constantly changing context' (Atkinson and Claxton, 2000: 6).

In what kind of language is this discourse expressed? This is problematic given that the knowledge we are talking about is largely tacit; much of what constitutes advanced professional practice is difficult to articulate. Sachs (2001) advances the idea of an activist identity that emerges from democratic discourses with emancipatory aims (ibid.: 157). This suggests that the language of this discourse is the language of teachers themselves as encountered in peer-to-peer exchanges and professional self-narratives. These are the 'symbolic systems used for such social purposes as justification, criticism and social solidification' (Gergen and Gergen, 1988: 20–21), 'the glue for collective professional identity and the provocation for a renewal of teacher professionalism' (Sachs, 2001: 158).

The 'masterliness' discourse: the Masters in Teaching and Learning

A version of this discourse was developed by the UK government for England with the short-lived introduction of a Masters in Teaching and Learning (MTL). The assumptions behind this initiative was that 'top down' approaches linked to national strategies (to raise standards in literacy and numeracy for example) were not having the anticipated impact on raising educational standards. There was an acceptance that reflective practice, as outlined by Schön (1983) and Kolb (1984) supported by communities of practice (Lave and Wenger, 1991), could have an impact on student outcomes.

Introduced by the New Labour government in 2007, the MTL signalled the intention that teaching would be a Master's led profession (Sorensen and la Velle, 2013: 77). This set a new benchmark for advanced professional practice that centred on the concept of 'masterliness'. Whilst this word is not found in current dictionaries it has entered the discourse of professional development as 'a state of advanced professional critical thinking linked to action and informed by research and evidence' (la Velle, 2013: 7).

The nearest noun to masterliness is 'masterly' which means 'showing great skill, (being) very accomplished' (Oxford English Dictionary online). The promise of a master's led profession had a positive impact upon the validation of teacher expertise and raising the professional identity of teachers. The 'masterliness' discourse built on the discourse of the autonomous professional and gave it greater validity through engagement in academic study and the theoretical evaluation of practice. The ambitious intention behind the MTL was that all teachers at some stage in their career would engage in practice-based critical enquiry (DCSF, 2008). However, there were counterarguments to this intention; Burton and Goodman (2011) articulated concerns that the MTL would promote standardised approaches to post-qualification teacher education and that ensuring that all teachers are exposed to largely the same professional development provisions would lead to greater state control of the education system.

The managerialist discourse

The impact of neo-liberal policies on education, heralded by the Education 'Reform' Act of 1988, saw the introduction of the principles of the 'free market'. Managerialist discourses and ideologies introduced into educational bureaucracies, as well as schools, viewed education as a commodity provided by schools with children, and more importantly parents, as the consumers or 'customers' (Ward, 2013). The managerialist discourse is based on two claims: that efficient management can solve any problem and that practices appropriate for the conduct of private sector enterprises can also be applied to the public sector (Rees, 1995). This discourse has impacted on notions of advanced professional practice in two main ways: through the introduction of performance management and the introduction of standards for teachers.

Concerns about raising standards of achievement and obtaining the best possible return from the resources that are invested in education predated the 1988 Education 'Reform' Act. In 'Better Schools: a summary' (DES, 1985a) concerns were raised about the quality of teaching which led to proposals that LEAs should be required to appraise the performance of their teachers. Subsequently in 'Education Observed 3: Good Teachers' (DES, 1985b) HMI articulated the constituents of good performance by teachers in primary and secondary schools. These included minimum expectations (being reliable, punctual, cooperative and willing), qualifications, personal qualities (a calm attitude and the creation of a climate of purpose), having a variety of teaching approaches, the ability to differentiate and motivate students and control classes, planning and assessment, maintaining professional relationships outside the classroom and engaging in extracurricular activities.

The creation of the Teacher Training Agency in 1994 introduced teaching 'standards' or competencies that defined not only what was expected of teachers in order to be able to enter the profession but also what was required by them in order to progress. Whilst these stages of progression cannot be seen as a model of expertise (Goodwyn, 2011) they do acknowledge and describe stages of advanced practice. In 1997 the idea of the 'advanced skills teacher' was introduced, a concept that originated from Australia and to this was added the stage of 'excellent teacher' in 2006.

By 2009 the standards for teachers in England and Wales outlined a progression route for teachers that went through several stages:

- Achieving Qualified Teachers Status (QTS) (i.e. initial training)
- Passing induction and achieving the core standards (i.e. probation)
- Post-threshold (meeting standards that warrant progression to a higher pay scale)
- Excellent Teacher
- Advanced Skills Teacher

The highest level of progression, the Advanced Skills Teacher (AST), is described in the guidance as essentially a career and reward stage (Goodwyn, 2011). This reflects the intention to provide teachers with a career pathway that allows them to progress professionally without having to take on management or leadership responsibilities. 'Good' teachers now had the possibility to develop their careers as leading practitioners who can have an impact on school improvement, supporting and encouraging the quality of teaching in others.

Similarly the position of Excellent Teacher provided a career route for those teachers who wanted to stay in the classroom but did not necessarily wish to engage with directly supporting other teachers. Interestingly this position received a negative reaction from the teaching profession who felt that the scheme and the title were potentially divisive.

The accountability discourse

Alongside the managerialist discourse, and complementing it, is the discourse of accountability as represented, in England, by The Office for Standards in Education (Ofsted), the body responsible for the inspection of schools, colleges and providers of initial teacher education. This discourse is given separate attention from the managerialist discourse because, although their intentions are undoubtedly similar, the accountability discourse uses very different and quite particular language. The terms that have been used to describe teaching quality have gained very specific meanings, which are informed by explicit criteria.

From the outset, when Ofsted was established in 1992, the framework made judgements on the quality of teaching. Initially there were seven different levels of judgement from 'excellent' (1) to 'very poor' (7) with evaluation criteria for each level and descriptions of what 'good' (3) and 'satisfactory' would look like. The framework was subject to continual revision and greater detail was added to the criteria, by 2003 the characteristics of teaching and learning were provided for levels 2–6, with short statements providing indications for awarding levels 1 and 7. The additional guidance for awarding level 1 was that 'difficult ideas or skills taught in an inspiring and highly effective way indicate excellent teaching' (Ofsted, 2003: 73).

In 2005 revisions of the framework reduced the number of levels from seven to four: outstanding, good, satisfactory and inadequate. There is no direct correlation between teacher expertise and being judged by Ofsted to be 'outstanding'; however, these criteria have had an impact on notions of what teacher expertise might look like. This has not always had a positive impact on classroom practice with the criteria driving formulaic approaches to classroom practice as teachers strove to ensure that they were 'ticking the boxes' when observed. The continual revision of the framework is often influenced by these patterns of behaviour, recent versions of the framework places a greater emphasis on the ways that teachers respond to students during the lessons and the extent to which they adapt their lesson plan according to the needs of the class they are teaching.

There is no doubt that the Ofsted inspection framework and the criteria that delineate what 'good' and 'outstanding' practice have had a direct influence on the ways schools understand what advanced pedagogic practice looks like. Whilst some schools will follow these descriptions slavishly and expect common standards and practices to be consistently applied in all classrooms others see this approach as being stultifying, preferring teachers to bring their own individuality to their practice.

The globalisation discourse

The final discourse that has a contribution to make to our notions of advanced professional practice is derived from the impact of globalisation on education. Globalisation is an ambiguous and contested concept which is viewed as being either beneficial (Friedman, 2006) or as a form of 'global pillage' (Giddens, 1999) in which the spread of global capitalism increases global inequality and destroys environmental resources.

The most significant impact that globalisation has had upon education is the increased competition between national systems of education within the context of a global 'knowledge economy' (Shields, 2013) in which the success of an education system is linked to economic prosperity. This competition is reflected in and driven by international tests designed to measure and compare educational achievement in different countries. Of particular importance have been the Trends in Mathematics and Science Studies (TIMMS: www.ttms.bc.edu) and the Programme for International Student Achievement (PISA: www.oecd.org/pisa/). Both TIMMS and PISA have ignited debates on educational policy and practice and have encouraged politicians and researchers alike to seek to learn from, or borrow, 'best practices' from other countries.

Organisations such as McKinsey and Company have produced reports in response to data on 'the world's top performing school systems', notably 'How the World's Best School Systems Stay on Top' (Barber and Mourshed, 2007) and 'Closing the talent gap: attracting and retaining top-third graduates to careers in teaching' (Auguste et al., 2010). Significantly these reports emphasise the importance of teacher effectiveness 'the quality of an education system cannot exceed the quality of its teachers' (McKinsey and Co., 2007). This represents an important shift away from views that argue for the primary significance of leadership in debates concerning school effectiveness and improvement. The principle contribution offered by the globalisation discourse is the reinforcement of the idea that the effectiveness of the classroom teacher is seen as the most important controllable feature of an education system. 'The world's best-performing education systems make great teaching their "north star"' (Auguste et al., 2010: 5). This discourse has played an important part in raising the importance and the profile of issues surrounding what constitutes 'great teaching'.

Chapter summary

This chapter has provided a summary of the different ways in which professionalism has been understood within the context of education and how the changes in understanding have been informed by social and political imperatives. This has in turn influenced the different ways in which advanced professional practice has been comprehended and described. The globalisation discourse has established the need to understand what constitutes 'great teaching' as an international priority, heading the agenda for educational debate across all countries.

Whilst managerialist and accountability agendas have played a part in seeking to bring about improvements in the quality of teaching they have had limited success and it is now widely accepted that it is not possible to mandate the shift from 'good' to 'outstanding'. There is therefore a need to establish a meaningful and critical understanding of advanced professional practice, without this it becomes impossible to create a long-term framework for professional development. Furthermore there is a critical issue regarding the recruitment and retention of teachers. Sustainable approaches to the development of professional practice are essential if any meaningful attempt is to be made to tackle these, and other, issues.

Establishing the status of teachers as professionals is an important priority and this needs to acknowledge what teachers actually do in the classroom. The concept of the improvising teachers is based on an understanding that classroom practice is complex and that teachers' work within dynamic and interactive contexts, which are situated and constantly changing.

This requires the exercising of professional judgement and knowledge that, as well as 'knowing that', involves 'knowing how to', drawing on both explicit and implicit (tacit) understandings. Teachers are engaged in complex responsive processes in which the capacity for adaptation is a key skill.

Any reconceptualisation of professionalism needs to be based on an understanding that pedagogy is fundamentally an improvisational and relational practice informed by dialogic teaching. The advancement of professional practice needs to eschew ideological frames and be seen through the lens of the growing research into expertise and expert performance. Improvisation (a significant factor in pedagogy and expertise) is understood as spontaneous, in the moment creative action that is informed by tacit knowledge and intuition and arises out of the dynamic interaction between fixed, non-negotiable structures and informal emergent structures. These ecological concepts provide the basis for outlining sustainable long-term frameworks for professional development, outlined in Chapter 9. The next section of the book provides a view of the improvisational nature of expert teaching derived from an empirical research project.

PART II
The empirical research: The improvisational nature of teacher expertise

5 The impact of school culture on the development of advanced professional practice

Introduction to the empirical research

The research that forms the basis of this study contributes to a growing evidence base that supports the anecdotal view that improvisation is a facet of expert teaching (Hattie, 2009; Goodwyn, 2011; Sawyer, 2011). Improvisation is a hidden aspect of expertise as in many cases it is replaced by other terms. For example, this aspect of expertise is sometimes referred to as the 'craft knowledge' of teaching:

> ... that part of their professional knowledge which teachers acquire primarily through their practical experience in the classrooms rather than their formal training, which guides their day-to-day actions in the classrooms, which is for the most part not articulated in words, and which is brought to bear spontaneously, routinely and sometimes unconsciously in their teaching.
>
> (Brown and McIntyre, 1993: 17)

The empirical research that is reported in this book was designed to explore the nature of the relationship between improvisation and teacher expertise, to observe what this looks like in practice and to understand the extent to which the teachers perceive their practice as improvisatory. The objective of this research was to critically challenge and extend existing notions of teacher expertise and advanced professional practice. The key research question was 'what is the relationship between teacher expertise and improvisation?' and this was supplemented by three further questions:

1. What are the cultural factors that determines the nature of expertise in particular settings?
2. To what extent do teachers perceive themselves to be experts?
3. How is teacher expertise displayed in the classroom and in what ways do teachers improvise?

A small-scale empirical study was undertaken between November 2011 and January 2014 in order to address these questions. A comparative case study methodology was employed in order to compare and contrast 'the particularity and complexity of a single case, coming to understand its activity within important circumstances' (Stake, 1995: xi). A qualitative methodology was chosen as an appropriate way to explore the participants' understanding and practice of improvisation given the subjective nature of this phenomenon. Qualitative research is inherently subjective and sees no need for the establishment of control groups in order to produce knowledge claims that have validity. Whilst it is not possible to claim that the conclusions arising from this research are generalisable, they do offer what is called *exemplary* knowledge (Thomas, 2011) in which the knowledge – insights and theory derived from this research – can be viewed and understood from the readers perspective, i.e., from within the context of their own knowledge and experience.

A pilot study was undertaken in one school, focusing on the case of one teacher. Following this study the sample group was extended to involve six other experienced teachers working in four other secondary schools in the South West of England. The selection of each participant followed a common procedure. An interview was held with the headteachers in each chosen school, who were approached as the gatekeepers for the research. Once they had given permission for the research to take place within their schools, each headteacher was asked to give their understanding of expert teaching and then asked to identify a teacher that met that definition. A meeting was arranged with those teachers to outline the purpose of the research and to ask for their agreement to participate. Having obtained their informed consent, each teacher was interviewed at the outset of the research and then observed teaching five lessons. Each lesson was followed by a post-observation interview to elicit their understanding of what had been observed. Constant comparative methods of analysis were used to draw out themes from the data and these were then used to create a grounded theory of teacher expertise (Charmaz, 2006).

Ethical considerations

From the very outset ethical considerations were given serious attention, and the design and practice of this research was undertaken within the bounds of the British Educational Research Association Guidelines (BERA, 2018). All the principle stakeholders were informed at the outset of the intent and purpose of the research and informed consent was obtained from all participants; there were no hidden or covert objectives. All of the participants were at liberty to withdraw from the research at any time and any accrued data regarding them would be destroyed. The research design acknowledged a responsibility to ensure the physical, social and psychological well-being of all the research participants. In the event that participants shared personal information a discussion took place to decide whether this information should be included in the research and how it would be reported. As this research was undertaken in a school setting the issues surrounding the well-being of the students observed were fully in accord with the ethical and moral responsibilities of the researcher in a professional teaching role. A final debriefing meeting took place with all of the teacher participants in which the general findings of the research, at that point in time, were shared with them for their comments. The names of the schools and all of the participants' identities have been anonymised through the use of pseudonyms.

Analysing the data

The data that was collected fell into two broad categories: audio recordings of semi-structured interviews and field notes of lesson observations. A decision was made not to record the lessons on audio or video in order to minimise the impact of the researcher being in the classroom and to minimise the stress on the teachers. All of the interviews were fully transcribed and then subjected to a process of initial coding utilising gerunds to detect processes and to keep the codes close to the data (Glaser, 1978) and to generate fresh ideas about the data (Charmaz, 2006). A second stage of analysis involved looking for connections between the initial codes, comparing data sets from the different teachers, grouping the codes in order to create categories or focused codes that can then be tested against the data. In the third phase of analysis the focused codes are related to each other within a conceptual framework, the process of theoretical generation. It is these codes that give rise to the grounded theory; a conceptual account of what is happening within the data. Further information on the construction and nature of the grounded theory is given in Chapter 7.

The data: interviews with headteachers

The data obtained from interviews with the headteachers provided insights into the relationship between leadership, school culture and teacher expertise. The decision to interview the headteachers came about when trying to resolve the issue of how to select the sample of expert teachers who would be asked to participate in the research. One approach to selecting the sample would involve establishing a set of criteria, derived from the literature review, in order to identify suitable participants. However, this strategy was problematic: what would happen if the teachers who agreed to participate did not meet some or all of these external criteria? An alternative approach would involve asking each headteacher to articulate their understanding of expert teaching and for them to suggest a teacher (or teachers) that met their criteria.

The latter approach was taken and this decision proved to be significant. Rejecting the use of external criteria to determine the sample highlighted the importance of context as a determinant of teacher expertise. It drew attention to the role that school culture has on informing and supporting teacher expertise and opened up a potential line investigation into the ways that professional development is socially constructed. The process of collecting data therefore began with establishing what is meant by school culture, the ways in which headteachers influence that culture and how this informs their views of teacher expertise.

Understanding school culture

School culture, at one and the same time, is easy to recognise but difficult to express in words. A number of terms are used to describe it: climate, ethos, the 'special qualities' of a particular school, 'the way we do things around here' (Bolman and Deal, 1997). School culture 'expresses itself in the signs and ceremonies in the school, the way that schools conduct assemblies, define roles and responsibilities and display learning' (Stoll et al., 2003:120). Culture is one of the most complex and important concepts in education (Stoll, 1998), which has suffered from neglect. Schein (1985) defines school culture as 'the deeper level of basic assumptions and beliefs that are shared by members of an organisation that operate unconsciously and that define in a basic "taken for granted" fashion an organisation's view of itself and its environment'. The culture of a school will therefore have a significant impact on the kind of teaching that takes place and, in turn, it will inform the ways in which teacher expertise is understood. The construction of the culture of a school, and the ways in which this happens, predetermines and provides the context for the social construction of teacher expertise.

The culture of any organisation cannot be looked at in isolation as it is the product and consequence of several other factors. Principally it is determined by its relationship with two other closely interrelated concepts: structure and power. The expression and distribution of power in an organisation is informed by specific values, beliefs and ideologies that, in turn, determine the structures that are put into place. Structures can either rationally determine what people in the organisation can do through high levels of social control or they can provide freedom to act in response to decisions that are taken. Cultures differ according to the extent that they control actions or permit a greater degree of autonomy. Capra (2002) articulates this relationship as the dynamic interplay between two kinds of structures: 'design structures', the formal, fixed and non-negotiable structures of an organisation and 'emergent structures', the fluid and informal structures created through informal networks and communities of practice. The art of leadership can be seen as the attempt to achieve a balance between design and emergent structures in order to create a culture that is effective and productive. This process is described by Habermas as the creation of a 'lifeworld': the social world where social actions and interactions occur and where subjects arrive at common and mutual understanding through communicative action. The lifeworld has three structural components: culture (the stock of knowledge on which people draw), society (the social norms that regulate institutional order) and personality (socially developed capabilities and skills). It functions through providing a context for action, a stock of shared assumptions and background knowledge, of shared reasons on the basis of which individuals may reach a consensus. The lifeworld is a force for social integration that is in opposition to 'the system', the world of instrumental and strategic action that is ideologically driven by economics and political power.

The relationship between design and emergent structures, and between the system and the lifeworld, is dynamic. The tension that arises from this relationship is, as explained in Chapter 2, is a significant driver of improvisational activity. This insight into the nature of culture informs a postulate of the research:

> that as all cultures are concerned with, and defined by, the relationship between fixed and emergent structures they are therefore improvisatory in their social nature and constructed being.

The improvisational nature of school culture affords school leadership with the potential to control or modify the culture that they inhabit. Hatch describes this process as 'a system of intersecting meanings to orient themselves to one another and coordinate their activities' (2011: 22), suggesting that culture is, in a way, the repository for symbols and artefacts its members produce, also the product of their collective sense making and the context in which meaning is made and remade.

School culture and teacher expertise: the headteachers' perspectives

The interviews with headteachers explored their views of school culture, how they have attempted to shape it and how it informs their views of expert teachers. The five headteachers who participated in the research were asked how long they had been in their current post, what was their previous experience of headship and their assessment of the culture of the school at the time of their appointment. Unsurprisingly their assessment of school culture was expressed with reference to Ofsted criteria (the inspection framework in England). Pseudonyms have been used for the headteachers and the name of their schools. A summary of this data is presented in Table 5.1.

On school culture

With the exception of William, all of the other heads at the time of their appointment saw changing the culture of the school as a key priority. Alan, Charles, Ben and Derek each gave examples of the ways in which their actions were critical in signalling the kind of culture that they wanted to develop. These stories illustrate the significant role that the headteacher has in determining and influencing the culture of a school and how this plays out in practice.

68 *The empirical research*

Table 5.1 Summary of experience of headteachers interviewed

Name of Head and School	Years at Current School	Previous Headship and for How Long	State of School at Start of Headship
'Charles' Wordsworth Academy	13	Yes: 5 years	Critical: 'would fail an Ofsted inspection'
'William' Shakespeare Community School	15	No	'Good, with outstanding features'
'Alan' Geoffrey Chaucer School	10	Yes: 3 years	'At quite serious risk'
'Ben' Milton School	3	No: but had been deputy head at Milton School for 3 years prior to being appointed as head	'coasting'
'Derek' The Blake School	15	Yes: 3 years	'coasting'

Alan described an incident that had occurred when he visited the school prior taking up his appointment. He saw eight students being forced to stand with their faces to the wall because they had refused to go to a detention.

ALAN: *So I actually went into the hall, I had no role whatsoever in the school at the time, and I said to the assistant headteacher 'can I have a word with those children?' I sat them down and asked what the situation was and I'm so glad that I did it. Boy, it sent shock waves through the school!*

The 'shock waves' related to the expectations he had about the ways he wanted students to be treated: that he did not want to see them humiliated and that he saw the need to build trusting relationships between staff and students.

Similarly Charles, in the early days as headteacher, went down to the place where the smokers hung out:

CHARLES: *Word went round and by the end of an hour the whole school knew that the new head had been down to where the smokers were. Nobody had been down there because it was so bad. So you start to do things and this immediately begins to change the culture.*

Both of these incidents, which in one sense are small events, had a significant impact in that they signalled that the status quo of the school was going to be challenged. Ben's approach to changing the culture at The Milton

School was through leading by example, modelling the qualities that he expected to see in his staff. He was very keen to promote a culture whereby teachers would feel secure in taking risks, not playing safe in their approach to teaching, and he set an example for this by experimenting with different approaches to organising the school day.

Derek at The Blake School was engaged in a long-term commitment to changing the culture of the school. This was a continual process that he sustained throughout his tenure. His intentions were articulated within a number of documents (prospectus, staff handbooks and policy documents); the key themes can be summarised as follows:

- A central focus on the student (placing the student at the centre of all that the school does)
- Relationships (the most important relationship in the school is between the teacher and the student and the primary function of those with a management responsibility is to support this relationship)
- Collegiality (for all staff the most important concept is collegiality: 'as professionals we are all equal, have an equal voice and are trusted')
- Shared understanding and expectations ('an organisational culture which involves shared understanding and expectations between, or of, all participants')

Evidence that these intentions are expressed in practice can be found in the report of the Ofsted school inspection of The Blake School undertaken in 2009. The report noted that both teaching and support staff enjoy working in this very inspiring creative atmosphere with opportunities for regular, motivating professional development, that they have a common sense of purpose because of the collegial style of management and that the strategies that teachers use in their lessons are very effective because they allow students to be actively engaged in their learning.

An analysis of the transcriptions of the interviews with the headteachers reveals the characteristics of school culture that were common to all of the schools:

- the creation of local conditions (a lifeworld) within which statutory and policy requirements (the system) were played out in a meaningful manner;
- a focus on relationships across the school, primarily on the relationship between teachers and students ('at the centre of all we do');
- recognising the importance of collegial relationships amongst the staff based on trust and permitting a degree of autonomy;
- the promotion of teaching and learning that encourages risk taking and reflection;
- making it acceptable for teachers to acknowledge when they are having problems.

On expert teachers

The key characteristics of the culture of the Blake School were directly reflected in the description Derek gave of an expert teacher (his actual words are given in italics).

For Derek the qualities found in an expert teacher are so simple:

For a start you have to really like children. It's about working with, not working on. Every time you walk into a classroom you have to establish a relationship where the child is important. Everything is around the advancement of learning.

The human aspects of being a teacher were really important. Expert teachers are able to create *an immense empathy, their humanity is at the forefront of all they do.* He also valued the importance of having a sense of humour *the other thing that is really at the heart of it, the most important thing after love is laughter.* Whilst subject knowledge is important it needs to be accompanied by the ability to see things through the eyes of the student *of being able to go back to square one*, to be able to relate the learning to individuals and to know how far students can be pushed. *The expert teacher knows where to stop that pushing, knowing the boundaries and then just going a little further each time.* The importance of 'pushing at boundaries' also applied to expert teachers who needed to have the personal ambition to be better than they were the day before.

For Derek the key qualities of an expert teacher can be expressed through having a commitment to building relationships with students, being empathetic and having the determination to continually strive to be better. The personality of the teacher was also very important to him. The teacher that he identified to be part of the research ('Anne') was valued because of her *total humanity and warmth, everything she is as a human being.*

William found it difficult to relate to the term 'expert teacher' and had resisted using it in his school as he felt that it was a hierarchical concept that conflicted with ideas of collegiality. His view was that very few teachers are experts in every aspect of teaching but that certain teachers develop expertise in particular areas. Other heads expressed different views of what they thought an expert teacher was. Alan emphasised the importance of self-awareness:

ALAN: *I actually think that an expert teacher is someone who is very self aware, they are almost a self expert because, in my experience, I think that those teachers that struggle are often people who are not really in touch with themselves. They don't* come across to the children as being complete or whole ... that there's a person standing in front of them.

Charles thought that having emotional intelligence was a priority and that this should be supported by strong subject knowledge. He thought that having subject knowledge was *pretty useless unless you have a really good understanding of how children learn, how people learn* and that in order to do this you need the emotional intelligence to build relationships: *if the kids like you and listen to you, they'll enjoy learning about the work for you.* Expert teachers are able to create a culture in their classroom where the kids know what to expect and they know it's about learning and they know they are safe. They know they are going to learn.

Ben saw expert teachers as having an absolute passion for their subject, able to constantly enthuse their students and to create a sense of *awe and wonder*. They are also passionate to ensure that every child makes progress.

BEN: *so they know the children inside out, they know their strengths and weaknesses, they know their background, where they've come from. They don't accept a one size fits all. They are determined to focus right down on individual students and to provide high-quality learning opportunities for every student they come across.*

He also noted the significance of the culture of the classroom: *the classroom culture is very important, that sets the tone.*

On improvisation

The headteachers readily acknowledged the importance of improvisation for teachers and they saw this as being related to teacher expertise. The personalisation of learning, for example, was seen as being as essential way to engage all learners and this required teachers to adapt to what is happening in the classroom.

BEN: *I think you've go to know the subject so well that you can be flexible and think on your feet and adapt to what they are coming back with or where they are going ... you need to be confident to allow children to lead.*

The ability of teachers to be perceived as co-learners within a classroom situation was viewed as a powerful quality that developed a mutual respect between teachers and students. Ben considered this to be a high level skill: *you've got to have a very professionally secure footing to be able to do that. I think that's where all teachers should get to.*

William recognised the importance of improvisation, which, for him, came about through responding to the needs and previous learning experiences of a class of 30 students: *things never go quite as you planned.* The situation that he described was one that demanded a teacher to be creative: *now I suppose that you can plan creativity but you can't plan improvisation.* He went on to explore this idea in greater detail.

WILLIAM: *Because if you are saying that improvisation is about having to work with whatever you are given then you might find that on an individual level in the lesson ... because a child has not understood something in the way that you had thought they were going to understand it or that they are in an emotional state that you hadn't predicted that they were going to be in. The teacher that is able to improvise will be able to think (they probably won't even think about (it) just responding automatically in a way that) okay, this isn't what I was expecting, I just can't plough on with what I was going to do, I have to respond to what I am given. So that might happen on an individual level or it might be (with) the whole class. I think we all know as teachers that something that works on one occasion won't work on another occasion because the class, for whatever reason, there is a collective mood which is completely different. They've just come from a wild lesson, maybe the winds blowing, maybe they're dreaming, maybe it's the end of the day. So I think that good teachers improvise in the sense that they take that as a given and then respond accordingly. A bad teacher will say 'I planned what I was going to do, it's all going wrong! Help!'*

Alan's view was that the ability to improvise comes from having confidence in the classroom, which then allows the teacher's personality to come through. Confidence might be the consequence of a number of things: the intellectual ability of the teacher, the amount of time they have been teaching or the depth of their subject knowledge. He considered that expert teachers were those who were aware of being 'in the moment' and able to respond to the events that are happening around them: *of all the things I have said* (in this interview)... *that has been the nugget! Because if you are there in the moment and the child is kicking off, you are there for them and they sense that you will be able to give them a bit of time.*

Charles had a clear view on the relationship between improvisation and expert teaching.

CHARLES: *... improvisation is one way of putting it, intuition is another. If you are formulaic, no matter how well you do it, eventually the kids are going to say 'oh no, we know what can happen' so you can't do that and also, because you are dealing with individuals, they will have different responses. Different situations arise so you have to be spontaneous. And you have to be intuitive and decisive and therefore I suppose you've got to improvise sometimes.*

On teacher autonomy

A characteristic shared by all of the schools was the high value that was placed on relationships and the acknowledgement that teaching is a relational activity. Prioritising the relational dimension of teaching has implications for other aspects and characteristics of school culture, one of which is seen in the need to empower teachers through permitting them to have a degree of autonomy. Derek's commitment to promoting the collegial culture within the school led him to empower and trust teachers in accordance with the priority of placing the child/student at the centre of all they do.

William was very clear that the culture of The Shakespeare Community School was concerned with placing relationships at the heart of all that they do, articulating the link between collegiality and teacher autonomy.

WILLIAM: *and we combine that with distributed leadership, so basically we let people get on with the job. We're not at all bureaucratic. So we don't say you must plan lessons in this format, we don't say we want to see your lesson plans. We are very laissez-faire in that respect. We don't tell them how to run their departments but we look to the results. So we provide a framework, we provide the support and we are rigorous on the outputs.*

William stated that in order to achieve outstanding results, and to encourage outstanding teaching, *you needed to release people's creativity*. However, he also acknowledged that whilst this approach may be appropriate *for certain staff that have been in the culture for a long while* it may not be appropriate for new members of staff. This approach could allow too much variation in practice and, if this was the case, there was a need *to pull people back towards a common baseline and then release them again.* He makes an important point here that autonomy needs to be earned and that it is related to having a sound understanding of the culture of the school.

The headteachers' views: a summary

The interviews with the headteachers established the importance of school culture and the significant roles that they played in shaping it according to their own values and beliefs. These views directly informed their view of expert teachers, acknowledging that the ability to improvise was important in that it enabled teachers to relate and respond to the needs of the students and express their humanity. In a school culture where, as Derek puts it, *'the child is at the centre of all we do'* then improvisatory teaching becomes an essential skill and teachers need to be afforded a degree of autonomy. What is implicit in the view of school culture that has emerged from the interviews with the headteachers is that the trust and respect for teachers provides them with the permission to improvise within their practice. Within the mindset of the school, influenced by the headteacher, personalised, creative responses to the individual needs of the students is not only desirable or acceptable but is essential if the aims of the school are to be achieved. Interestingly the teachers who participated in the research invariably commented on the importance of the headteacher in establishing the culture of the school and how this had influenced the way that they taught.

A further aspect of school culture that was not mentioned by the headteachers became evident during the time spent observing the teachers. Subcultures, created by teachers themselves, were acknowledged as being very important and provide further insight into the ways in which teacher expertise is socially constructed.

The importance of subcultures

Charles drew attention to the significance of the culture of the classroom and this draws attention to an important point about school culture. School culture is not a single entity but is comprised of a number of subcultures, multiple lifeworlds that emerge out of communities of practice. A subculture can be defined as a group of people within a culture that differentiates itself from the parent culture to which it belongs, although often maintaining some of its founding principles, a space for democratic participation and living:

> fostering (the) moral development of participants, individual and collective identity formation, positive emotional bonding and thus solidarity and rational critical thinking in learning.
>
> (Hairon, 2021)

The development of subcultures by expert teachers in their own classroom was an interesting phenomenon that arose from, and was directly influenced by, the degree of autonomy that they were given to teach in their own way. At times these subcultures might be at variance with the standards and norms that were generally applied across the school to other teachers. However, the efficacy of their teaching, demonstrated in their examination results and the progress that their students achieved, gained them permission to teach in their own way. This idea will be explored in greater detail in the next chapter; however, what is particularly important at this point is to note the headteachers acknowledgement, and support for, this practice.

Charles commented on this in the following way. *The culture of the school allows the expert teacher to create the right culture in their classroom.* He also made the point that he encourages the personalisation of practice, that he doesn't want teachers to be the same. *The kids don't like it. They don't want to go from one* (expert teacher) *to another ... to another. They want to go from a really good lesson to a really good lesson to a really good lesson.*

This statement suggests understanding the culture of the classroom as an example of a subculture created within the context of the overall culture of the school. Whilst maintaining and reflecting many of the characteristics of the culture of the school there is the idea that the teacher is encouraged to make the culture of the classroom their own, differentiating it from other classrooms through the ways in which they personalised the space and their practice.

Understanding the importance of the subculture of the classroom led to an awareness of other subcultures within the school. These were created by teachers, had their own distinctive characteristics, and they contributed to the social construction of teacher expertise. One such location was the departmental resource room or shared office space. The following extract from my field journal captures the important features of this space at The Milton School.

> **Box 5.1**
>
> Events are happening all around me. Staff enter and leave the room, conversations happen. Teachers are marking books, sharing information about students and pick up on details (knowledge of students) that they didn't know about. Students also are allowed into this room, either to use the computers or to do some photocopying. There is a sense that this is a shared space.
>
> I reflect on the importance of this space for the English team. It is clearly 'theirs', a space that they inhabit and can work in, an alternative to the shared staffroom which functions more as a social space. The room is untidy but there is also a sense of organisation and purpose. Each teacher has a desk space that is their own, there are shelves and worktops where sets of text books are stored. There are facilities for making coffee; a fridge, a sink, a kettle.

Barbara (the expert teacher I observed at The Milton School) explained that this departmental office space was *extremely important*. She spends most of her time in this room when she is not teaching engaged in a range of activities: marking work, preparing lessons, sharing resources, sharing information about students, providing space for students to work if necessary. All members of the English department share and use this room and the head of department has an adjoining office. This room offers a safe 'offstage' space for all the members of the English department. I asked Barbara how the culture of this shared space helps her as an expert teacher.

BARBARA: *The department I am in is very strong and supportive. This is first and foremost a factor in my success. I can walk out and say 'I don't know how to do this' and often a less experienced teacher can come up with a good idea. There is no shame in that: asking for help, seeking assistance, asking for ideas.*

At The Shakespeare Community School a similar space was provided for the Science teachers. Harry (one of the teachers I observed) noted the importance of this space.

HARRY: *The people in Science are so nice ... it's important to have adult company. The office culture is really lovely, they bring in cakes etc. but there's an awful lot of learning going on, informal stuff ... so important to me in my early years. They are mutually supportive, not just in the science department, that's something the management are really good at.*

One of the key findings of the research is that any attempt to understand the improvisational nature of expert teaching has to consider the issue of context.

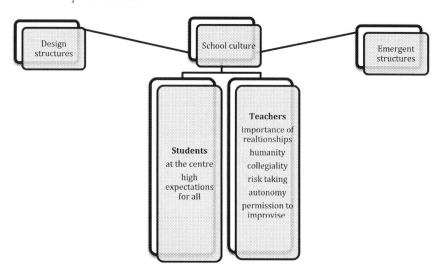

Figure 5.1 A model of school culture

The interviews with the headteachers illustrate the impact that school culture has on views of expert teaching and that advanced professional practice is a situated phenomenon. The practice of individual teachers has to take into account the context in which they work. The research findings offer a view of school culture that can be described as the 'lifeworld' of a school, that emerges from the dynamic interplay between fixed and generative structures and, as such, is an inherently improvisational environment. A theoretical model of school culture is shown in Figure 5.1.

Chapter summary

This chapter outlined the methodology of the empirical research and reported the findings gained from interviews with the headteachers. The significance of school culture when researching teacher expertise was explained. Establishing the culture of their school was seen to be an important priority for all the headteachers and examples were given of the ways in which they had an impact on shaping it. Their view of school culture directly informed their understanding of what it meant to be an expert teacher and they valued the ability to improvise. Teachers were seen to need a degree of autonomy given that teaching is a relational activity and expert teachers were seen as those that were able to understand the emotional climate of the classroom and intuitively respond 'in the moment' to the needs of their students. The significance of subcultures within the school was highlighted, particularly those spaces where informal conversations can be held and where teachers can ask for help when they might be facing difficulties. These spaces make an important contribution to the social construction of teacher expertise.

6 Teacher perceptions of expertise and improvisation

Introduction

This chapter presents the findings of the research from the perspective of the teacher and shows how their expertise is demonstrated in the classroom and the perceptions that they have of their practice. Seven teachers were interviewed and observed in five secondary schools in the South West of England. The following short pen portraits serve to introduce the participants to the reader. Pseudonyms have been used for each teacher and the schools in which they work.

The participants in the research

Anne trained in Law and Paralegal Studies in the United States where she also worked as an attorney. She has been a teacher in the UK since 2000 teaching English and Law and for most of her career has taught at *The Blake School*.

Barbara has taught English and Media Studies at *The Milton School* for 12 years, and this is the only school she has taught in. She was appointed as a newly qualified teacher (NQT) of English and subsequently has taught Media Studies. She is second in charge of the English Department.

Helen has taught Modern Languages at *The Wordsworth Academy* since 1994 and she is currently an Advanced Skills Teacher with the remit to support the quality of teaching and learning in her own school as well as other local primary and secondary schools.

Eleanor has been teaching for 30 years and has spent 20 years at *The Geoffrey Chaucer School*. She is a member of the senior leadership team and is an Assistant Headteacher with a responsibility for teaching and learning. She teaches Media Studies.

Harry, John and Richard all teach at *The Shakespeare Community School*.

Harry is a Science teacher who came to teaching after a career as a research scientist where he gained a PhD. He trained as a teacher when he was 34 and has been teaching at the Shakespeare Community School for six years. This is the only school he has taught in.

John is a Drama teacher and has been at The Shakespeare Community School for three years. This is the first school he has taught in. He has a

78 *The empirical research*

background in professional theatre and before becoming a teacher he worked in theatre in education.

Richard is Head of Drama and Director of Arts at The Shakespeare Community School and has taught at the school for 8 years and has over 20 years' experience working in schools. He is a Specialist Schools and Academies Trust lead practitioner for Drama and has co-written a book on how drama can promote authentic learning in secondary schools.

Perceptions of expert teachers

An initial interview with each of teachers explored their perceptions of what the term 'expert teacher' meant and how they related to this concept. Their words are shown in italics. As has been previously noted, the term 'expert teacher' is not commonly used within educational discourse, partly because teachers do not like this word when it is applied to teaching (Goodwyn, 2011).

Anne, for example, displayed a reticence to using this term; *I don't think I'm an expert*. Not only did she not see herself as an expert but also she did not want me to use this term when I talked to her colleagues on my visits to the school. We agreed that a suitable compromise would be to call her 'an established teacher'. Anne was however able to outline the qualities that she thought defined an expert teacher: *a mutual respect of staff and students, a good sense of humour, subject knowledge and relationships with colleagues.*

Barbara recognised the challenge of being an expert teacher, emphasising that it is about continual improvement: *it's a tall order, it's someone who is learning the whole time, already thinking about the next lesson to ensure the progress of all children. I don't think that there is a tick list of what makes an expert teacher in terms of solid proof ... there is more of a reflective approach.*

The importance of reflection in order to improve your teaching was also important. This included taking ideas from other people *and manipulating them to your own benefit* (Barbara) and having an open mind about the way that you teach. An important characteristic of expert teachers emerged as a disposition to pro-actively seek opportunities to further their professional development.

HELEN: *I don't think that anybody can ever be an expert teacher but I think you can be an aspiring expert and I think that denotes knowledge and skill. I think that one of the things that I learnt as I became a teaching and learning coach is that you have to be proactive in seeking that knowledge and that can help you to develop your skills ... I will spend the rest of my teaching career probably continuing to develop that knowledge and then practising those skills so I can actually develop my practice towards expert. Like I said, I don't think I'll ever get there. I don't think anyone can ever get there because there is always more to learn, there's always more to develop and the job changes so often.*

Whilst Harry did not think that the term 'expert teacher' was one that he would use about himself, he saw an expert as someone who had a) good subject knowledge and b) was good at getting it across to young people (pedagogical content knowledge). He said: *you can be good at b) with a little of a).*

Perceptions of expertise and improvisation 79

You need to be a good people person, to cajole, inspire and enthuse. To be a true expert you would bring the two together. He didn't think that there was one approach to becoming an expert, *no golden bullet* as he put it, as he thought it was important that teachers were able to modify what they were doing according to the needs of different students. He also identified the importance of humour (*I do try*), honesty (as to why students were being asked to learn certain things), challenge (teaching should provide students with *an opportunity to manipulate a concept in their brain*) and inclusive (*being interested in the kids in the middle, the invisible ones who are experts in not being spotted*).

The view of 'the expert teacher' that emerges from these interviews is that expertise is seen as a process of 'working towards' becoming a more effective teacher as opposed as a state that you arrive at. This reflects Stacey et al.'s (2000) concept of a transformative teleology in which human actions and interactions are seen as processes that move towards a future that is under perpetual construction. There is no mature or final state, only a perpetual iteration of identity, difference, continuity and transformation.

These teachers were self-motivated to improve their practice and in doing so valued the opportunities to learn from colleagues and to share their experience. The importance given to learning from others, within a community of practice (Wenger, 1998), indicates how expertise is socially constructed within the ecology of a school.

In common with the headteachers' views there was a considerable emphasis on developing skills in the relational aspect of teaching. For the teachers this meant knowing the students as individuals, having high expectations for everyone, creating a positive atmosphere in the classroom based on mutual respect and being able to adapt what is being taught in order to engage all students. Having the interpersonal skills to enthuse, inspire and motivate students was seen as being critical.

All of the teachers who participated in the research were asked to come up with a 'headline' statement that summarised what expert teaching was all about for them. These statements are shown in Table 6.1.

Table 6.1 'Headline' statements summarising what the term 'expert teaching' means.

Name	'Headline' Statement
Anne	*knowing the backstory, that's what expert teaching is all about*
Barbara	*that's the nature of expertise, it's the dialogue in the classroom*
Harry	*enthusiasm* (for the subject).
John	*relationships with the students*
Richard	*what experts do is bring a technical element to classroom practice, the technical (teaching) skills and associated subject knowledge. Selling it to students is another skill, to communicate why and demonstrate how. Expert teachers I have come across have both skills*
Eleanor	*high expectations for all*
Helen	*my philosophy is just making people feel comfortable in my classroom, feeling that they are worth something. I can develop their confidence and make them feel worthy as human beings*

Table 6.2 'Headline' statements grouped under the three themes of teacher expertise

Theme	Supporting Statements
Relationships	*knowing the backstory, that's what expert teaching is all about relationships with the students*
	Selling it to students is another skill, to communicate why and demonstrate how
	I can develop their confidence and make them feel worthy as human beings
Dialogic teaching	*that's the nature of expertise, it's the dialogue in the classroom*
Climate for learning / culture of the classroom	*enthusiasm* (for the subject).
	what experts do is bring a technical element to classroom practice, the technical (teaching) skills and associated subject knowledge.
	high expectations for all
	my philosophy is just making people feel comfortable in my classroom, feeling that they are worth something

An analysis of these statements identified three themes, common practices that expert teachers are able to do and that other less-accomplished (novice) teachers may find challenging. These practices are: expertise in building relationships, expertise in dialogic teaching and expertise in creating a culture for learning in the classroom. The 'headline' statements are grouped under these three headings in Table 6.2.

The next section of this chapter explores these three themes in more detail by drawing on the data gained from lesson observations that focused on the ways in which these teachers displayed their expertise in the classroom. The themes of building relationships and dialogic teaching are looked at together as they are so clearly related, explored through an extended account of Anne's teaching. This narrative text, constructed from field notes and presented as third-person continuous prose, (Cohen et al. 2011) provides a clear illustration of the connection between relationships and dialogic teaching. This is followed by an account of how expert teachers create a unique and personalised classroom culture.

Expertise in relationships and dialogic teaching: Anne, a case study

Anne's expertise is demonstrated in the way that she builds relationships with her students through using a pedagogy that prioritises dialogue and discussion. Her approach to building relationships with her students is based on the principle of wanting to know them as individuals. She clearly likes the students that she teaches and she places importance on *knowing the backstory* of each student and her interactions are based on having knowledge of their parents and carers, siblings and other family members that she has taught or who have previously been at the school. This considerable pool of knowledge has been built up over the ten years that she has been teaching at The Blake School. She says *you can read them* (the students) *like a book; that's what we are talking about when we talk about expert teachers.*

Her familiarity with the students is particularly noticeable in the sixth form classes that she teaches, no doubt due to the maturity of the students and the fact that she has taught many of them before. However, the kind of interactions she had with sixth form students were also observed when she was teaching younger students.

The beginning and ends of lessons provide Anne with important opportunities to engage with the students and she shows an interest in what they are doing outside of school. She stands by the door of the classroom and greets each student with a *how are you*, often developing this into a brief conversation about what they had been doing since the last lesson. If a student asks to talk to her after the lesson she readily agrees to this.

Anne is also prepared to share appropriate information about herself as a person, and this process of self-disclosure makes the building of relationships a two-way process. She presents herself as a 'human being' as opposed to 'just' being a teacher. This quality is acknowledged by her headteacher who said he valued *her total humanity and warmth, everything she is as a human being*. Anne creates an informal atmosphere in the classroom in which students are expected to work hard. She uses humour to maintain interest in the lesson or to manage minor behaviour issues and plays up her American background through the deliberate use of Americanisms when she talks to students (*sweetie, honey pie*). Her body language is informal, she often sits on the corner of her desk and she talks with her hands. She generates a warm non-threatening atmosphere that then allows her to challenge the students in their learning.

Anne's core pedagogic practices are dialogue and discussion and this is linked to and follows on from her interest in, and like for, her students. She teaches in this way because she enjoys talking with them, and this strategy is common to all the classes that she teaches. She takes every opportunity to engage the students in the lessons, encouraging them to share their opinions and ideas. This was observed in a sixth form English class studying 'The Great Gatsby', presented in a case study below, in which her expertise in building relationships with the students and her ability to teach dialogically are skilfully combined.

Case study of Anne: The Great Gatsby lesson

Prior to the lesson Anne explained to me that on the previous day the Sixth Form students had attended a road safety event organised by the Police, designed to encourage young drivers to take care on the roads. The event included graphic descriptions of road accidents, and she was aware that this would have had an emotional impact upon the students, including the class that she was about to teach. She re-designed the start of her lesson to capitalise on their response to this event and to use this as a way of informing their understanding of 'The Great Gatsby' (one of the key incidents in the novel being a horrific car crash).

(Continued)

> As the students entered the classroom, they were handed a post-it note and were asked to write their response to the road safety event. The notes were then stuck on a wall and a student was asked to read them out. Whilst she was doing this Anne summarised the points on a white board and then asked the class to make connections between the words on the board and 'The Great Gatsby', one student replied 'it's like the car crash in the novel'.
>
> This led into the main activity of the lesson that was designed to help the students prepare for an assessed presentation at the end of the term. She had prepared a PowerPoint presentation; each slide contained a number of quotations from the novel and was used as a basis for discussion. Anne provides guidance on the vocabulary that the students will require if they are going to do well: *you need to use words like 'lexus'.*
>
> Slide 4 contains a number of quotes about the character of Gatsby, and she asks all the students to think about each quote. She then chooses three students to give their thoughts, and they do so in turn. She then brings in other students to add their contributions, building up ideas, developing the themes that emerge. She gives positive feedback as they share their ideas: *Very good! Yes, very good!*
>
> The next slide contains further quotes about Gatsby. *These are really difficult quotes, they get more difficult as they go along.* As she raises the level of challenge in the lesson so the engagement of the students increases. They start to pick up on other points that they consider to be important, building on ideas, spotting contradictions in earlier ideas, developing their own line of thought. The lesson has become a form of collective thinking in which all of the students were contributing to the dialogue.

What had the students learnt from this lesson? In the post-observation interview Anne considered that they had made progress in their understanding of the text, developed higher order vocabulary, glimpsed at hidden layers of meaning, explored symbols and themes used in the novel and prepared for their assessed presentations. My perspective was that the lesson, once it had begun, developed a momentum of its own in which learning emerged from the dialogue between the members of the class. The lesson did not adhere to notions of a 'well-structured lesson', yet it had the quality of an event where significant learning took place.

This view of the expertise inherent in building relationships and dialogic teaching leads into looking at the expertise inherent in developing the culture of the classroom, drawing on the observations of the other participants in the research.

Expertise in developing the culture of the classroom: the lifeworld at a micro level

One of the key ways in which teachers demonstrate their expertise is through the ability to create a unique and personalised culture within their own classroom. This process can be understood by drawing on Habermas's theory of communicative action that makes a distinction between the lifeworld (where communicative action takes place) and the system (defined by power and money where strategic and instrumental action holds sway).

The previous chapter looked at the ways in which the lifeworld informed the construction of the culture of the school and this was described as the lifeworld developed at a macro level. Teachers in their classroom operationalise the same processes when creating the conditions where there is a mutual and common understanding between them and their students that facilitates shared action. These conditions arise from what Habermas refers to as communicative action:

> the interaction of at least two subjects capable of speech and action who establish interpersonal relations (whether by verbal or extra verbal means). The actors seek to reach an understanding about the action situation and their plans of action in order to coordinate their actions by means of agreement. The central concept of interpretation refers in the first instance to negotiating definitions of the situation that admit of consensus.
>
> (Habermas, 1984: 86)

In Habermas's schema communicative action is contrasted with instrumental or strategic action where the attainment of ends may not be shared with other participants and may be concealed from them. Communicative action requires a level of authenticity and transparency that is achieved through trust, respect and a degree of informality in order to 'provide a repository of shared meanings and understandings, and a social horizon for the everyday encounters with other people' (Finlayson, 2005: 52). The shared meanings and understandings of the lifeworld provide a unity, but not a totality, in that it is open to revision and change.

The concept of communicative action is important to the way that the lifeworld of the classroom is understood. The lifeworld of the classroom cannot be established by the teacher alone but has to be jointly constructed with the students. This joint construction of the lifeworld occurs as a consequence of the previous two areas of expertise: relationship building and dialogic teaching.

However, it is unrealistic to expect that all aspects of classroom interaction can be negotiated with students. There are certain parameters, rules and boundaries that are non-negotiable (the design structures and the characteristics of the system). Consequently, this research makes a distinction between the *climate* of the classroom and the *culture* of the classroom. The term climate is used in relation to those aspects of the classroom that are controlled and directed by the teacher (derived from strategic and instrumental action), whilst the term culture is used to refer to the shared beliefs and social behaviour of both the teacher and the students within the classroom situation (derived from communicative action). The expertise of the teacher is demonstrated through their ability to engage the students (and themselves) within the learning process, moving towards establishing authentic relationships based on equality and trust.

All of the teachers observed had clear procedures for establishing the climate for learning within their classrooms, those aspects that are controlled and directed by the teachers: the non-negotiable design structures. This was particularly noticeable in the decisions that were made regarding the beginning and the end of lessons. They all had well-established routines that only differed to the extent that they were formalised.

Barbara had very clear and formal expectations that governed the start of all her lessons. As the students entered the classroom they sat in places determined by a seating plan and copied the learning objective and the homework that they would be required to do into their exercise books. This was undertaken in silence. A different approach was observed in Eleanor's teaching; she used background music to create a relaxed atmosphere. Many of the teachers used the start of the lesson, as the students came into the classroom, as an opportunity for humour. Other characteristics of climate setting included reminders about high standards of behaviour, demonstrating their trust and respect for the students and getting the students engaged in learning at the earliest opportunity.

Teachers also demonstrated their expertise in the way that they structured activities, embedding statutory requirements such as taking the register so that this did not disrupt or distract from the learning. Some teachers took the register once the lesson was underway, whilst others, Helen for example, used the register to engage with every member of the class. In her German lessons she spoke in the target language when she took the register and once the student had replied that they were present they had to answer a question (in German) based on the theme for that lesson.

The establishment of a culture of learning was seen in the ways that the teachers created the sense of a learning community which emphasised the social nature of learning. The cultural expectations were that the students would not just learn from the teacher, but they could learn from each other and, in turn, support the learning of their peers.

A good example of this was seen in a year 10 lesson taught by Barbara. One aspect of the students GCSE English examination is a speaking and listening activity, assessed by the teacher. The examination required evidence that the students could interrogate arguments, challenge assumptions and demonstrate sustained listening skills. Barbara created a lesson based around a balloon debate. All of the students had to select a 'character' and argue the case as to why they should be chosen to stay in the balloon instead of the others. Three students at a time went to the front of the class and, as their character, presented their arguments. The other students in the class, listening to the speeches, were encouraged to ask questions. This provided not only evidence of their own speaking and listening skills, but they were also encouraged to help others to improve on their target grades.

Engaging students in the learning was achieved in a number of ways. These teachers were adept at alternating between teacher directed activities and asking students to work in groups, pairs or individually. Having a variety of activities gave the lessons pace, time was used effectively with clear indications as to how long each activity was going to last, and different techniques were used to indicate when each activity was due to come to an end.

Dividing up the lesson into different activities reinforced cultural norms where learning was seen as a cooperative and shared activity. It also provided the teacher with opportunities to work with individuals, building relationships with students on a one-to-one basis. In a year 9 media lesson Eleanor established group tasks and then went round the class, targeting individuals who needed support. She made a particular point of working with one boy who was behind with his coursework as he had been away from school. Other students expressed their appreciation of this aspect of the culture of the classroom, stating that they liked the way that Eleanor '*didn't get in the way of the learning, we can just keep going*'. They also mentioned that she would always help if a student was stuck.

The expertise of these teachers was characterised by the ways in which they established a culture of learning that was inclusive and effective right across the ability range. In two cases, Barbara and Helen, I observed them teach classes that represented the most able students in the schools and other classes that contained some of the least able students. They adopted broadly consistent approaches for both groups, but they made sure that the learning was structured to a greater extent for the less able students in order to demonstrate to them that they were able to make progress.

A final, and important, characteristic of the culture of the classroom is the ability the teachers had to create a personalised lifeworld. The importance given to building relationships with students, knowing about their backstory and responding to them as individuals has already been noted. This was reciprocated by sharing appropriate personal information with their classes. This is an approach that is not without its problems, but the expertise of these teachers was demonstrated in the way that they negotiated this issue, establishing professional boundaries whilst letting the students know that they were human and that they had a life outside of school.

Barbara, in a year 11 media lesson, began talking about one of her favourite television programmes, 'Hollyoaks' and it was evident that this was a running theme with this class. A year 10 English lesson concluded with her telling the class about an event she attended with her husband for servicemen and women who were leaving the Army. She explained that each person who was leaving had an advocate who had to speak on his or her behalf. One advocate had been very funny whilst another had not been so coherent. She used this story to illustrate the importance of developing speaking skills in 'real-life' situations, but it also gave the class an insight into her life outside of the school.

In the post observation interview I asked her if she felt that it was important to talk about herself in this way.

BARBARA: *Well that's funny because I was thinking about that when we were talking earlier. When I trained I remember distinctly being told off about referring to my personal life in front of the class; that was seen as bad practice. But actually I find it really helpful and I do it a heck of a lot. I did it this morning with the year 10 class. I do it an awful lot because a) it makes it* (the learning) *relevant, b) it humanises me and helps the relationship* .

Barbara is aware that she can use these personal stories in different ways: the 'Hollyoaks' references, *it's a bit of a joke now …. it's my tap in* to connect with specific groups of students. Allowing the students to see her as a real person is also motivational, which she relates to the way in which she is motivated by her headteacher: *it helps you to come across as likeable and human, like the head. You are motivated by him because he is a human being. It's really important that you are not some kind of robot.* Sometimes she uses this as a way to deal with incidents of misbehaviour. In response to a sarcastic response from a student, she replied that she was not feeling that well herself today *but look, I bothered to come into school today.*

For Barbara the personal insights that she shares with her students are a helpful way of building positive relationships. Through sharing her humanity she is aligning herself with her students, illustrating her engagement with them in *a common cause.* Her expertise comes through in the way that she is able to judge what is appropriate, and what is not appropriate to share.

Chapter summary

In this chapter, we have looked at the ways in which the teachers who participated in the research viewed the concept of the expert teacher and the ways that this is demonstrated through their classroom practice. Whilst a degree of modesty might be the reason that they did not feel that they were experts, there was a shared view that becoming an expert was an ongoing process of continual reflection and improvement that could not be articulated as a definable end state.

Their expertise was formed around three core practices: the way that they were able to build positive relationships with students across the ability range, dialogic teaching and the creation of a culture of learning, a personalised lifeworld within their classrooms. The lifeworld of the classroom was founded on climate setting principles (determined by the teacher through non-negotiable routines and expectations) and a culture of learning that was co-constructed with the students, reflecting their knowledge of the students as individuals (*the backstory* as Anne called it) and reciprocated by appropriate personal insights into the teacher as a human, a 'real person'.

In the next chapter, the findings from the research are summarised in the form of theoretical models that outline the relationship between teacher expertise and improvisation that informs the concept of the improvising teacher.

7 The improvising teacher as a prototype of advanced professional practice

Introduction

This chapter provides an overview of the findings gained from the empirical research and presents them as theoretical frameworks. These frameworks not only summarise the characteristics of advanced professional practice but, beginning with the end in mind, they provide guidelines for developing a long-term framework for the professional development of teachers based on the prototype of the improvising teacher.

The grounded theory was generated in the following manner. Data gained from the research, in the form of observations of lessons and interviews with teachers and headteachers, was analysed using a constant comparative method. Interviews and field notes were transcribed and then subjected to a process of initial coding, utilising gerunds in order to focus on processes (Glaser, 1978), keeping the codes close to the data. The second stage of data analysis involved looking for connections between the initial codes, comparing data sets and grouping them in order to create categories or focused codes, which were refined and tested against the data. A third phase brought the focused codes together in a conceptual framework, a grounded theory (Savin-Baden and Major, 2013) which provides a conceptual account of what is happening in the data. Grounded theory, whilst not able to offer predictions or explanations of human behaviour, offers the possibility of going beyond narrative by demonstrating an understanding of the data at a conceptual level. The concepts that emerged from the process of analysis amount to an ecology of advanced professional practice in that all of the constituent parts are interrelated and interconnected as a complex and dynamic system that informs our understanding of the improvising teacher.

A grounded theory of the ecology advanced professional practice

The grounded theory of the ecology of advanced professional practice is shown in Figure 7.1. Each concept or component of the model is explored in greater detail and illuminated by insights drawn from the research data and literature.

DOI: 10.4324/9781003223207-9

88 *The empirical research*

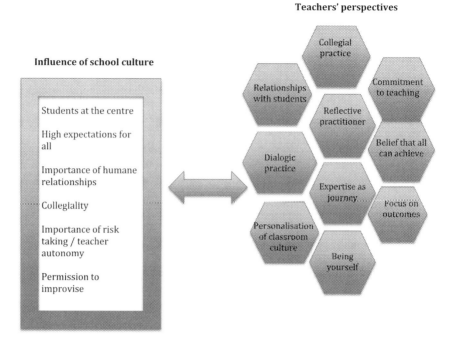

Figure 7.1 A grounded theory of the ecology of advanced professional practice

The teachers' perspectives are aligned against the influence of school culture as this is an integral aspect of the ecology of advanced professional practice. There is a reciprocal relationship between school culture and teachers in that whilst school culture has influence upon the teachers, teachers also influence and inform the culture of the school. The grounded theory of the ecology of advanced professional is determined by the teachers' perspectives and illustrates the congruence between culture and practice.

A central idea, shared by all of the participants in the research, is that progress towards **expertise is a journey**, a process as opposed to an end state. The teachers felt that they could never claim that they had 'arrived' as an expert teacher but that they were always working towards becoming one. This reflects the central proposition of a Transformative Teleology (Stacey et al., 2000), that human actions and interactions are processes that move towards a future that is under permanent construction. Whilst the emergent form of expertise is unpredictable, it is patterned according to the characteristics of relationships within the wider culture.

The process of becoming an expert was achieved through being a **reflective practitioner**, in which the teachers were continually reflecting on practice in order to introduce changes to their teaching. They engaged in a process of continual adaptation and 'tinkering' with their pedagogic strategies and they enjoyed experimenting with new ideas. They had the confidence to take risks, trying out new ideas in the knowledge that if it didn't work then they would have the ability to try something else. Habermas argues that critical/self-reflective knowledge produces an authentic learning that is beyond the *techne* (that of making and doing) if the goal of learning is to be one befitting being human and that this is the only truly assured, totally comprehensive and authentic form of human knowing. He identifies the cognitive interest of self-reflexivity as emancipation, becoming a free agent through praxis, the practical action for change. From an ecological perspective the capacity for adaptation is central to professional learning environments (Daly et al., 2020). Allied to this commitment to reflective practice is the engagement in **collegial practices**, sharing ideas and supporting the development of other teachers.

All the teachers demonstrated a **strong vocational commitment to teaching**, enjoying the 'nuts and bolts' of their work: preparing lessons, teaching and assessing students' work. This commitment was strengthened through their allegiance to the school that they worked in, acknowledging the correlation between their values and beliefs and those espoused by the school. In many cases, although not all, the teachers had spent a considerable part of their career in their school. This reinforces the importance of culture and the interaction between an individual's values and beliefs and the environment of the schools.

The teachers displayed an inclusive attitude to all the students that they taught, holding the **belief that all students could achieve.** All students were deemed to have worth and that they deserved the support and attention of the teacher according to need. Their practice was informed by an egalitarian outlook.

This was related to having a **strong focus on outcomes** and educational attainment, wanting all students to achieve the best that they can. They had a very detailed knowledge of the examination and assessment systems, both at a national level and school level. Whilst they gave great attention to academic achievement (driven by school policy and national accountability agendas), they were also committed to the human outcomes of developing students as individuals.

Their pedagogic practice was informed by establishing **strong professional relationships** based on a detailed understanding of the background of the students. This relationship is reciprocated through the teacher sharing appropriate information about themselves so that the students are able to relate to them as a 'real person' as opposed to 'just' being a teacher. These relationships were personalised to the extent that the teachers could **be themselves**. The importance of relationships also extended to the **relationships with their peers** who were seen as a source of support when they had problems and who provided ideas for reinvigorating their teaching. This draws attention to the ways in which 'practices, beliefs and values are constructed within the environment – how school cultures are constituted and enacted' (Milton et al., 2020: 4)

Teaching is grounded in dialogic practice, which is skilfully used to engage students in the learning process. Asking questions, generating discussion and group work contributes to the interplay between teacher directed activity and individual, pair and group work. Dialogism as a practice is at the heart of improvisation arising from relationships and interaction with students.

Finally these teachers were able to create a **culture within their own classroom** that encouraged learning. This was a personalised 'lifeworld' that acknowledged and reflected the culture of the school but also was characterised by their own values and beliefs. They were able to create safe and trusting spaces in which students could learn. As described by Habermas the lifeworld comprises three components: the stock of 'knowledge' on which people draw, regulatory social norms and socially developed capabilities and skills. The teachers were able to personalise the processes through which their students engaged with knowledge, create acceptable means for integration and equip their students with the motivation to see themselves as able to achieve.

The improvising teacher as an expert prototype

This grounded theory of the ecology of advanced professional practice advances the argument for seeing the improvising teacher as a prototype model of expertise. This is derived from a non-essentialist view of expertise that rejects the idea that advanced professional practice consists of well-defined standards that all experts will meet. In part this is due to the impact that context and school culture have upon advanced professional practice. Sternberg and Horvath advance the concept of the prototype as being that which 'represents the central tendency of all the exemplars in the category' (1995: 9) in which experts bear family resemblances to each other, and it is this resemblance that structures the category of 'expert'.

Evidence from the research emphasises the influence that context and culture play on what is deemed to be expertise and that the range of expert practices displayed by the teachers varies according to circumstance. This leads to the claim that advanced professional practice viewed from the perspective of expertise is best expressed as 'a teacher with a variety of expertise' rather than 'an expert teacher'. This acknowledges that teachers with expertise display a range of varied situated practices that have evolved through a continual process of development. Whilst such teachers will have much in common, they are not necessarily the same. The range of their expertise will not be seen to the same degree in all cases at the same time and as such supports the claim to adopt a prototype view of expertise.

The concept of improvising teacher can be illustrated through taking the components of the ecology of advanced professional practice and looking at them from two perspectives: the assumptions that inform their practice (the *mindset* of the improvising teacher) and their actual practice in the classroom (the *expertise* of the improvising teacher).

The mindset of the improvising teacher

The mindset of the improvising teacher can be explained with regard to four key areas:

- Perceiving expertise as a journey and not as an end state
- A predisposition to 'artful' improvisation through self-reflection and the continual adaptation of practice
- A commitment to teaching
- A belief that all students can achieve

One of the clear messages that came through from all of the participants was that the term 'expert teacher' is an unhelpful and inappropriate way of characterising advanced professional practice. This is due to a number of reasons: the teachers considered that this term made them 'stand out' from their colleagues; they were uncomfortable with this idea because they did not accept that they were an 'expert'. Their mindset was informed by the idea that expertise was something to be continually strived for and determined by 'what works best' within a particular context at a particular time. Their practice is based on the assumption that teaching is a complex and situated activity where it is not possible to know or predict what approaches will be effective.

A consequence of this was that they were continually open to find ways of adapting their practice and accepting the idea that there was always something else that they could learn. They were predisposed to self-reflection and asking others for help when things went wrong. Although they might not articulate it as such, they adopted an improvisational mindset.

A final and important aspect of the mindset is having a commitment to teaching, of enjoying the 'nuts and bolts' of preparing lessons, assessing work and supporting the development of all students. Part of this vocational commitment to teaching is a belief that all students can achieve.

The expertise of the improvising teacher

The second perspective concerns what teachers actually do in the classroom. The expertise of the improvising teacher is seen in a range of interrelated practices.

The previous chapter outlined three 'headline' areas of expertise that characterised the teachers' practice:

- building relationships with students
- dialogic teaching
- creating a personalised lifeworld in the classroom

Additional evidence derived from lesson observations, interviews with the headteachers and noting the impact of school culture adds the following practices:

- the adaptation of classroom practice both 'in the moment' and afterwards as a consequence of self-reflection
- establishing collegial relationships with peers that supports the co-construction of expert practices
- a focus on educational outcomes
- subject knowledge combined with detailed knowledge of examination and assessment requirements and processes
- an ability to relate to students through 'being yourself'

These expert practices are interrelated and they cannot be thought of in isolation. As has been seen in the case study of Anne's teaching a teacher that engages in dialogic teaching is, at the same time, building relationships with the students in their classroom. Focusing on the outcomes that they expect of all their students will inform reflection and the adaptation of their approaches to teaching, likewise a vocational commitment will of necessity want all students to achieve and in order for this to happen teachers will need to, and want to, get to know their students as individuals. Teachers that are continually reflecting on their practice and who are committed to collegial approaches will willingly share examples of good practice and seek advice from their peers. Each practice contributes to an ecology that is developed both formally and informally through communities of practice in which expertise is socially constructed.

Understanding expertise as being culturally situated is expressed in the first key postulate of the research which states:

> That as all cultures are concerned with, and defined by, the relationship between fixed and emergent structures, they are therefore improvisatory in their social nature and their constructed being.

The key practices of expertise are concerned with making decisions in real time, adapting approaches and responses according to the reactions and engagement of their classes. This is a creative process that relies upon the tacit knowledge that teachers have.

The argument for seeing the improvising teacher as an expert prototype is supported by research undertaken by Smith and Strahan (2004) based on Sternberg and Horvath's model and which employed a methodology similar to the one used in this study. Eschewing approaches that drew comparisons between novices and experts they looked at a similarity-based category of experienced experts and used a more naturalistic approach to the study of expertise in teaching. The 'family resemblances' that they discovered

Table 7.1 Comparison between the improvising teacher and Smith and Strahan (2004)

The improvising teacher as expert prototype	Six shared tendencies of expert teachers (Smith and Strahan, 2004)
Expertise as a journey	A sense of confidence in themselves and their profession
Continual reflection on practice	
Vocational commitment (to being a teacher and to school)	Talked about their classrooms as communities of learners
Inclusive attitude – seeing students as individuals	Maximised the importance of relationships with students
Focus on outcomes: attainment and achievement	Employed student-centred approaches to instruction
Building relationships: with students and peers	Contributed to the teaching profession through leadership and service
Dialogic teaching	Were masters of their content area
Creating personalised 'lifeworld' – classroom culture	

have much in common with this study and the similarities are shown in Table 7.1.

There is a significant overlap in the family resemblances that were identified in each study. Important similarities are seen with regard to the confidence that teachers have in themselves and the profession, the importance of relationships, seeing learning as a shared enterprise and the importance of student-centred learning. These similarities provide a very clear picture of the nature of teacher expertise. The differences, on the other hand, are interesting as they further our understanding of teacher expertise in four ways:

i. There is the continual reflection on practice, which results in adaptation and experimentation in their teaching. This, in turn, informs the idea that expertise is a developmental journey that does not have an end state.
ii. The teachers were very aware that one aspect of their expertise was shown in their efficacy in being able to ensure that all their students did well, or better than expected in national tests and examinations.
iii. Mastery of their content area (or subject knowledge) was an area that was taken for granted, and consequently was not discussed in any detail by either the headteachers or teachers. It was nevertheless seen to be important. An important and distinct area of knowledge was the detailed understanding that the teachers had of examination and assessment procedures, the processes through which student attainment would be measured. Acquisition of this knowledge enabled them to make judgements regarding the choice of examination boards and the best ways to prepare their students. This form of knowledge does not seem to be articulated within our current understanding of content knowledge, pedagogic knowledge and pedagogic content knowledge. The importance given to this is presumably a consequence of the accountability measures that all schools need to attend to and the introduction of target driven cultures.

iv. Finally an important feature of expertise was seen in the way that teachers were able to create a unique culture for learning in their classrooms, a personalised 'lifeworld'. The oppositional concepts of the 'system' and the 'lifeworld' as described by Habermas can be clearly seen in the experiences that teachers face when having to deal with the conflicts that can emerge between their own beliefs and values, the ethos of the school and the political and statutory demands placed upon education. An important characteristic of teacher expertise is that they are able to co-create with their students a 'lifeworld' within the classroom whereby a consensus is reached, a personalised space in which teachers and students can relate as individuals. Through presenting themselves as an authentic person they are able to create an environment in which students feel accepted, secured and valued. The lifeworld of the classroom is a holistic and unified space created by a teacher 'whose pedagogy is characterised by the integrity of a supportive relationship and best practice pedagogy as one action rather than two' (Osterman, 2010 cited in Lovat, 2013: 77).

How the research evidence supports the concept of the improvising teacher

Having derived the concept of the improvising teacher from the research findings raises the question as to whether the teachers involved in the study saw themselves in this way. Interviews with the participants provided insights into the relationship between expertise and improvisation and how expertise was the product of experience gained over a period of time. Barbara, for example, acknowledged that her expertise was derived from her experience of teaching, which enabled her to reach a point of automaticity in which she does things without thinking about them:

> *I think a lot of your experience over time becomes second nature. So whilst when I started I might plan lessons in great detail, write down every question I was going to ask, I think of these questions immediately now.*

Automaticity is one of the key characteristics of expert performance, allowing practitioners to access a broad repertoire of responses to situations and leads to Barbara to having the confidence to try different approaches and to take risks:

> *with experience there is less fear that things will go wrong and that it is OK to chuck an idea out into the open and run with it ... I think there needs to be an element of things coming on automatic pilot.*

Harry also agreed that there was a link between expert teaching and improvisation, but that experience was necessary in order to be able to improvise successfully. He specifically drew attention to having an experience of the longer time frames that were involved in teaching.

> *It* (improvisation) *can only happen when you know how long it's going to take to teach the course… You'd be brave to do it in PGCE or the first and second year of teaching. You need to go through the course a number of times.*

The experience gained from engaging with the longer time frames of the school year, for example the cycle of terms, the duration of exam courses and key stages, is important. Harry pointed out that this experience provides him with the knowledge of when it is appropriate to improvise or to allow the class to go *off on a tangent* and when he needs to focus on the priority of covering the exam syllabus. This suggests that whilst some teachers may display outstanding performance in the early phase of their career, expert practice may not be seen until after four and seven years working in schools (Day et al., 2006).

Richard's experience as a drama teacher informs the way that he responds to his classes. He explained that there was an expression that he often used: *I can tell from the sounds that you are making that the work is not going in the direction that I want it to go in.* His experience enables him to interpret the 'tones' or 'sounds' of the students in order to determine if they are on task or not. *Is that improvisation?* he asked *its changing direction I suppose but its reacting isn't it, whereas teachers who are less confident will let it run because that is what the plan is.* Richard said that he liked to plan his lessons but felt more confident to *take it in a different direction if the headteacher is not watching me!* His response is an important reminder of the distorting impact that lesson observations can have.

John also *definitely agreed* that there is a link between expertise and improvisation, considering that this was about moving away from the lesson plan.

JOHN: *I'm very strict with my planning but once I know what I'm doing I can then improvise slightly. If students need a bit more time then I can give it to them because I know where I can come back in. I won't lose the plot of the lesson or the arc where I'm going.*

He recognised that an important aspect of improvisation in the classroom was the way that it can bring about a shift in the power relationship between teacher and students.

JOHN: *If you have a strict agenda then it's your agenda, it's not the students agenda, its not what they want. If there is an aspect of the lesson that they want to explore in greater depth you've got to be prepared to take that step with them and allow them.*

He thought that this approach would not be acceptable for every teacher as some would be uncomfortable in deviating from what they had planned to do.

However, he thought that improvisation *is massively important ... it's the difference between teaching a student and showing a student* (what to do), meaning that improvisation is concerned with teachers engaging in a relational interaction with their students as opposed to simply showing or telling them what to do.

The evidence derived from the interviews indicates that improvisation was not only seen to be an important characteristic but that it was a positive and desirable aspect of teaching and associated with teacher expertise. The ability to improvise is dependent on experience, of having greater confidence in the classroom. This experience is shown by having a greater efficacy as a teacher, of having a wide repertoire of strategies that work across the range of students and understanding the longer-term rhythms of the school years and the examination cycles. Experience allows many of the routines of teaching and relating to students to become automatic, a part of tacit knowledge, which allows the teacher to 'sense' when and how to intervene, informing a range of professional judgements. The increased confidence that comes from experience allows teachers to take greater risks, knowing that if something doesn't work then they will be able to try something else to rescue the situation. The ability for teachers to be able to respond to the needs and interests of their students brings about a shift in the power relationship, making the students more active agents in the process of learning.

The concept of the improvising teacher is based on a number of assumptions. The first being that there is a distinction to be made between improvisation that is merely an 'off the cuff' response to a situation, the kind of improvisation that is referred to as 'flying by the seat of your pants' and a form of improvisation that is explicitly acknowledged as being part of advanced professional practice, arising out of experience and expertise. This is the distinction made by Quintilian between 'artless' and 'artful' improvisation. Artful improvisation within the context of teaching comes about through the acquisition of the two types of knowledge identified by Ryle (1945): 'knowing that' and 'knowing how to'. 'Knowing that' requires the development of a conceptual understanding of improvisation that includes an awareness of the different ways to approach improvisation and a critical awareness of what is required to improvise 'artfully'. This is conceptualised as being able to develop an improvisational mindset. 'Knowing how to' is concerned with acquiring an accomplishment in improvisational practice that is informed by experience and expertise. This is referred to as having a skillset of improvisational practice.

The improvising teacher can be defined as someone who explicitly engages in 'artful' improvisation, employing a pedagogy that is relational, dialogic, personalised and subject to continual adaptation. Expertise is viewed as an on-going process of professional formation driven by self-reflection and emerging from a community of practice. A self-conscious and articulated professional identity as an improvising practitioner is informed by the development of an improvisation mindset and an improvisational skill set. The developmental process of the improvising teacher is shown in Figure 7.2.

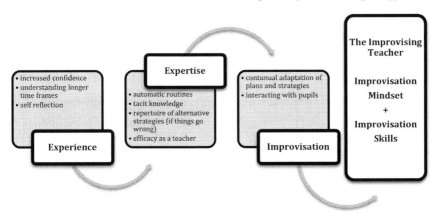

Figure 7.2 Developing the improvising teacher

Chapter summary

In this chapter the findings gained from the empirical research have been presented as theoretical frameworks to guide future action. A grounded theory of the ecology of advanced professional practice has been outlined, providing the conceptual foundations for the improvising teacher. The range of expertise is viewed from two perspectives: the mindset and the actual practices demonstrated in the classroom. The chapter concluded with the views of the research participants on what it means to be an improvising teacher and an outline of the developmental process that leads to this form of advanced professional practice.

8 The social construction of the improvising teacher

Introduction

This chapter concludes the overview of the findings gained from the empirical research from a theoretical perspective. These frameworks not only summarise the characteristics of advanced professional practice but, beginning with the end in mind, they provide guidelines for developing a long-term framework for the professional development of teachers.

This chapter looks at the findings of the research from an organisational perspective in which the school is viewed holistically, as a complex ecology. This ecology is considered from three viewpoints: structure, culture and power in order to provide insights into the social construction of the improvising teacher. Sternberg and Horvath (1995) argue that teacher expertise is variable, informed by a 'prototype' and one of the significant variables is context, the specific and situated formations of teacher expertise that are generated through a dynamic ecology. The components of this ecology, structure, culture and power, are interrelated. The culture of a school is influenced by the structures that are put in place, and decisions that are made regarding structural matters (and the resolve to enforce these decisions) are the consequence of power relations. The interrelated nature of these concepts is shown in Figure 8.1.

The three concepts of structure, culture and power operate at micro, meso and macro levels. For example, they apply to the teacher in the classroom, at a whole school level and at local/national level through the influence of local/regional authorities or national policies. Each of these concepts is discussed in turn drawing on both the literature discussed in Part I of the book and the views of the participants.

Structure

Structures within organisations define the parameters within which individuals work and interact with each other, determining what work is done and how it is done. Structures, as the essential defining characteristics of organisations, identify the boundaries between freedom and constraint, shaping

Improvising teacher as social construction 99

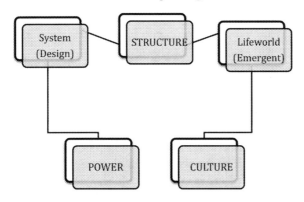

Figure 8.1 The school ecology: structure, power and culture

behaviour and social interaction. They are also important for the way in which we understand improvisation: as jazz musician Charlie Mingus succinctly put it 'you can't improvise on nothing, man' (Santoro, 2000: 271). Understanding the ways in which structures inhibit or enable improvisation is of vital importance as it emphasises that improvisation is the consequence of, and is generated from, structure, a view that is in contrast to assumptions that improvisation is inhibited by structure.

The relationship between structure and improvisation can best be understood by acknowledging Capra's distinction between 'design' structures and 'emergent' structures. As has been noted earlier these two types of structure reflect Habermas's concepts of the system and the lifeworld. This dynamic relationship not only generates improvisational activity but also has an impact on culture and the exercise of power.

The research shows that, at the micro level of the classroom, teachers refer to these two structural resources when they think about improvising: the 'fixed' structures represented by the lesson plan and the 'emergent' structures represented by the physical presence of the students in the classroom. These two areas are interrelated: responding to the needs of the students will necessitate adapting the lesson plan.

Whilst all of the participants acknowledged that the lesson plan was the key structural device that informed their teaching, the level to which they planned their lessons varied. Some teachers planned their lessons in meticulous detail, whilst others would have only have a sketchy outline of what they intended to achieve, experience had given them a sense of how to shape the trajectory of the learning. Experience gave them the confidence to improvise around the lesson plan in response to the specific needs of their students. The extent to which they did this was directed by their awareness of the constraints of the syllabus or the demands of a particular point in the school year. These factors determined the extent to which they could follow the needs and interests of the students or 'pull them back' accordingly. For some teachers, detailed planning was seen as a way in which the relationship with the students could be developed.

There are other structural factors that impact upon teaching and which need to be taken into consideration. The materiality of the physical space of the classroom is an obvious case in point. All of the teachers had a room in which the majority, if not all, of their lessons were taught. The way that they structured the physical space enabled them to determine their own approach to teaching. Helen, for example, arranged the tables in the room so that the students were sitting in groups, avoiding rows of desks that faced the front of the classroom. This suited her teaching style that moved between teacher-centred tasks and group work. Considerable attention was given to detail including the structuring of resources that were placed on each group of tables: dictionaries, pens and pencils, role cards and suggestion to help students if they got stuck. It was also noted how the structure of the physical space informed the culture of the classroom.

The way that time was structured was also a strong feature of the lessons that were observed. All the teachers made full use of the timespan of the lesson, making sure that students were engaged in learning as soon as they entered the room. Continually changing activities and the focus of the learning meant that the lessons had pace. Helen's lessons were structured through alternating between teacher-led activities directed at the whole class and individual, pair and group work. Group work was meticulously structured and each student was allocated a specific role to play in their group (this varied from lesson to lesson). Teachers also had their own way of 'counting down' – signalling that the time they had allocated to a particular activity was due to come to an end.

When the teachers were asked about the structures that were of particular significance to them they drew attention to the structures that were put in place at the meso (whole school) level that were designed to support staff to deal with disciplinary matters. Examples of these kinds of structures included strategies such as 'parking rotas' (a classroom where disruptive students can be temporarily removed to), a 'time out room' or the 'on call' rota where a Head of Department or member of the pastoral team can be called to intervene and resolve disciplinary issues within the classroom. These systems were deemed to be important because they provided a sense of security for the teachers in the decisions that they made:

HARRY: *A teacher can put a line in the sand and you'll be backed up.*
HELEN: *Teachers are not having to deal with everything themselves.*

The structures that are put in place to support and reinforce good behaviour have an impact on students (making them aware of the expectations that the school has and codes of conduct) and on staff: *teachers know what is expected.*

When Eleanor was asked for her views on the importance of structure, she reflected on the overall structure of schools, noting that they have not changed significantly since the 19th century in spite of the changes that have taken place in society and the culture of young people.

ELEANOR: *The industrial structure of schools,* (perceptions of schools as exam factories), *the kind of thing that Ken Robinson was talking about in 'Changing Educational Paradigms'* (Robinson, 2010); *the fluidity, the ideas such as gifted and talented year 7 students learning alongside year 10 students hasn't really come about. The industrial structure that he talks about hasn't changed.*

Eleanor went on to talk about a blog by Tom Sherrington (headguruteacher.com) that she recommended as a source for new ideas: *he's very forward thinking yet he is moving towards tighter structures.*

This discussion with Eleanor highlighted two contradictory views about the overall structure of schools. On the one hand, there is the argument that schools need to be restructured in the light of the changing needs of society and in response to the greater understanding of the ways in which people learn. The counterargument, driven in part (though not entirely) by government policy, is wanting to see schools as being structured on so-called traditional lines providing young people with clearly defined structures to compensate for the lack of a stable home background. The solution to resolving this contradiction, suggested by the findings of this research, is that structure needs to be viewed from the dual perspective of the fixed, non-negotiable design structures and the fluid inter- and intra-relational generative structures. The art of leadership is to get the balance right between these two approaches.

There is a close relationship between structure and culture. Structures define the culture of a school to the extent that they are a tangible expression of what Schein (1985) refers to as the deeper level of basic assumptions and beliefs that are shared by members of an organisation, that operate unconsciously and that define in a basic 'taken for granted' fashion an organisations view of itself and its environment. The priority for the headteachers who wanted to change the culture of their school was to get the structures 'right'. This might mean changing the structure of the leadership team or the school day, adapting the curriculum or setting new expectations for learning in lessons.

Culture and context

One of the significant findings from the research was that the culture of the school was deemed to be extremely important to the teachers that were interviewed; as Gu and Day (2013) point out, 'conditions count'. What is it about the culture of a school that sustains and motivates these expert teachers? What are the factors that made them want to stay teaching at the school? What role does the culture of a school play in the process of professional maturing?

The concept of culture can be defined as:

> a pattern of shared basic assumptions that was learned by a group as it solved its problems of external adaptation and internal integration, that has worked well enough to be considered valid and, therefore, to be taught to new members as the correct way to perceived, think and feel in relation to those problems.
>
> (Schein, 2004: 17)

This definition draws attention to the ways in which culture is socially constructed. The 'pattern of shared assumptions' can be seen in the importance that was given by some of the participants to the match between their values and beliefs and the culture of the school. This alignment influenced their commitment to stay at the school and the longevity of their service played a significant part in the acquisition of experience, which, as has been seen, is a crucial factor in the development of expertise. The length of time required to gain a level of expertise emphasises the crucial importance of teacher retention. The headteacher has an important part to play in this and clearly can have an influence on retaining the teachers that they valued. As Helen pointed out *'every time I thought of leaving Charles found me another job to do'*.

Other teachers commented on the significance of the impact that the headteacher has on school culture. A common characteristic of that was noted in the schools visited was the focus that was given to high achievement, creating an environment for learning where it is not deemed to be *'geeky' to be seen as bright*.

A culture of high achievement extended to the teachers as well. One participant noted that *'teachers cry if they get 'good' from Ofsted and not 'outstanding'*. Alongside this aspect of school culture was a more nurturing dimension in which teachers are supported and not criticised if they are having problems and that they would receive help and advice to resolve any difficulties that they might have with particular classes or individuals. Helen had a specific role in the school as an Advanced Skills Teacher with the remit to support staff who were having difficulties. This was organised on a system of self-referral and was not reported back to the headteacher. The headteacher was only involved if decisions needed to be made about changing the responsibilities or working conditions of the teacher in order to support their development.

A further influence on the culture of a school is its context, which is determined by the geographical location, the social context and the cultural norms expressed by the students. Eleanor commented on this with particular reference to developments in technology.

ELEANOR: *The student world has changed over the past 10 years. Notions of what it is to be British have changed; things are much more fluid. Values and ideologies are in a state of flux. This is a challenge to me as a digital immigrant. (Technology) moves in a very fast way.*

The culture of each school was also directly influenced by its catchment area. Given that the majority of the schools in the sample served predominantly middle class areas, this had an impact on the generally positive attitudes to school that the students held.

One of the most important findings of the research, as has been already mentioned, is the expertise involved in creating the lifeworld of the classroom, a negotiated culture within which learning can take place. The expertise involved in this concerns the co-creation of a space for learning that is not only shaped by the teachers expectations, beliefs and values but also engages with the expectations, values and beliefs of the students. As a mutually comprehended shared space for learning the lifeworld of the classroom becomes a personalised 'culture within a culture' that reflects the wider cultural assumptions of the school but expresses them in a specific and personal way. This is achieved through acknowledging and responding to the personal and lived experiences of the students, adapting the teaching in the light of a detailed understanding of *'the backstory'* as Anne put it. Alongside acknowledging the students as individuals, the teacher finds appropriate ways to share their own personal beliefs, values and experiences. The extent to which this becomes a coherent and mutually accepted construct allows both students and teachers to create a meaningful learning environment in which the imperatives of the 'system', at a national policy level and school level, are played out in terms that are mutually agreeable. The teacher becomes a credible expert at shaping and forming the conditions in which learning can take place. The classroom becomes a space in which external demands are modified and adapted in order to create personalised and shared lifeworld.

A headteacher's perspective on this point was expressed by Charles: *And maybe that's what an expert teacher does: they create a culture in their classroom where the kids know what to expect and they know it's about learning and they know they are safe. They know they are going to learn.*

There are a number of examples from the data that illustrate the ways in which this happens. Andy, for example, thought it was important that he should *'tell the truth'* about what the students are learning: whether this was purely for the purpose of passing an exam or whether it had wider relevance of how this will be of value later on in life. He thought that it was important that he should be explicit about the more instrumental aspects of learning and that students should understand why they were being asked to do certain things.

One aspect of the ways in which teachers created a personalised culture in the classroom was that they modified, or in some cases ignored, school rules in the light of their own values and beliefs. One teacher shared the following with me: *I'm out of order sometimes. You* (the students) *are meant to walk in, stand behind your desk and then sit down. I can't do that! Kids get on to the fact that each teacher is different.* This point illustrates that there is a fine line between the personalisation of the classroom culture and adhering to the expectations of the culture of the school as a whole. The tension between these two positions is an issue of power and this is explored in the next section.

Power

Having a degree of expertise infers a level of knowledge, understanding and experience and this confers a level of power. This section of the chapter looks at some of the ways in which structure and culture informs the power that expert teachers have, how it is displayed and the implications of seeing teacher expertise as fundamentally improvisational. Does this undermine or enhance the power that teachers have? This book claims that teacher expertise is principally grounded in the relationships formed between teachers and students and that teaching and learning is personalised according to the knowledge that the teachers have of their students and the knowledge that they choose to share about themselves. This suggests a relationship in which a teacher's power is not imposed upon students but arises out of the relationship between teacher and students.

Insights into the relationship between knowledge and power and the way that it informs the relationship between teacher and student can be obtained by looking at Habermas's theory of knowing, a theory that 'impels the kind of reasoned and compassionate reflection and self-reflexivity that results in benevolent action' (Lovat, 2013: 70). Habermas identifies three different kinds of knowledge, each of which is impelled by a different cognitive interest (the ways that knowledge serves different purposes).

Empirical/analytic knowledge serves the purpose of technical control; *historical/hermeneutic knowledge* serves the purpose for understanding meaning, (a communicative knowledge resulting from engagement interrelationship and dialogue) and *critical/self-reflective knowledge* serves the interest of being emancipated and becoming a free agent.

Habermas argues that critical/self-reflective knowledge produces an authentic learning that is beyond the *techne* (that of making and doing) if the goal of learning is to be one befitting being human and that this is the only truly assured, totally comprehensive and authentic form of human knowing. By acknowledging the subjective nature of knowing in which 'facts are never given in isolation from the minds that received them' (Ferre, 1982: 761), Habermas shows an interest in the way that the mind works in constructing reality. The 'critical/self-reflective' form of knowing has an emancipatory intent in which our autonomy as a knower will make us reflect critically on our subject matter, our sources and ultimately ourselves as agents of knowing.

The theory of knowing can be applied in an educational context to analyse teacher-learner relationships and the implied power structures within those relationships (Lovat, 2013). This is outlined in Table 8.1.

The relationship between the different types of knowledge and teacher/student relationships provides a useful framework for looking at the kind of power that teachers with expertise have. An obvious place to start is to identify the ways in which teachers with expertise have the ability to establish a culture for learning in their classroom. This attribute is valued by headteachers as well as by peers. One headteacher referred to one of the participants

Table 8.1 Analysis of teacher-learner relationships and power structures in relation to Habermas's three kinds of knowledge

Type of Knowledge	Empirical/Analytic	Historical/Hermeneutic	Critical/Self-reflective
Relationship between teacher and learner	Teacher as subject knowledge 'expert'	Partnership/shared power	Role reversal: teacher as learner and learner as teacher
	Learner as novice	Communicating about meanings and negotiating understandings	Learner free to think own thoughts. Relegation of power from teacher to learner who has confidence and power to control own learning.
Pedagogy	Didactic	Dialogic	Dialogic + personalisation of pedagogy

in the research as being able to *get the students eating out of her hand*. What is implied in this statement (and which was supported by evidence gained in the lesson observations) was that students across the entire ability range were able to make progress in their learning in this teacher's lessons. What was made explicit by this comment was a perception of the power that the teacher had over all the students that she taught. Additionally, recognition by the headteacher conferred power on to the status of the teacher.

The power relationships that were observed between teacher and students were not gained by coercion, both in the particular instance referred to above and in all other cases. The language used by teachers when talking about these relationships referred to concepts such as 'respect', 'trust' and 'love'. Two processes were identified by which power was demonstrated in the classroom: power 'over' the student by the teacher (exercised chiefly to ensure that the students were engaged in learning) and empowerment 'of' the students through dialogic processes that engaged them as active participants in the learning process.

The power that teachers had 'over' their students was derived from several factors: the status and experience that the teachers had within the school, their knowledge and ability to control classroom behaviour and their personality. Their approach to managing behaviour was based on treating students in a respectful manner.

The empowerment 'of' the students occurred through more general factors, principally through realising the cultural expectations of the school that were expressed by the headteachers in terms such as '*working with as opposed to 'on' students* (Derek), not tolerating staff shouting at students (Charles), tackling the resentment that students feel towards being treated unjustly (Alan) and believing that all students have the potential to be successful.

The teachers that were interviewed and observed shared these assumptions, believing that the best way to teach was to involve the students in the learning process. Their vocational commitment to teaching as a profession and their interest in the students that they taught meant that their pedagogy was driven by a desire to engage the students in dialogue and hear what they had to say. It is this engagement with dialogic pedagogies that brings about a different power relationship with students.

The teachers did not explicitly talk about their understanding and awareness of power in the post-observation interviews so this issue was raised in a final interview in which they were specifically asked for their views on this concept.

Eleanor felt that her style of teaching involved handing over a great deal of her power to the students. She stated that this did not necessarily imply a loss of control. For her this approach made her question how much power teachers had and highlighted the paradoxical nature of power in the classroom.

ELEANOR: *Actually, as a teacher you don't have any power at all, only expectations. You can't make any student do anything. The punishment thing doesn't work; it's about the things that you expect. If you go in* (to the classroom) *in a power type mode you are treading very dangerous ground with some students. The trick is to getting them to think that they are in control.*

In effect she was making a connection between having power 'over' and the empowering 'of' students in which the former is achieved through the latter. She rejected an approach based on coercion as being unworkable.

One of the characteristics of the power that teachers have 'over' their students is that it is derived from having the confidence to 'be themselves'. This is expressed through sharing information, opinions and experiences that they have had in order to provide their students with a view of them as a real person. The research suggests that this is a reciprocal arrangement that arises out of the teacher wanting, and needing, to know the students as individuals and which, in turn, leads them to share (appropriate) aspects of their own lives. Implicit in this approach is the encouragement of a more mutual power relationship within the classroom. The ability to achieve this seems to be a significant aspect of teacher expertise.

ANNE: *The power relations in the classroom, it's a mutual thing. The more mutual it is the more success that you have. If the students don't feel that they are empowered then I don't think they will make progress. They need to have a degree of power over their own learning, or power to feel free to explore, to make progress.*

What this seems to suggest is that the strength of the lifeworld of the classroom and the ability of teachers to be able to create this with their students, is critical. Being able to develop the social world of the classroom, where learning occurs through social action and interaction, which is seen as a shared action that is bound by mutual respect, has an impact on the learning that takes place. These conditions shift the kind of knowledge that is generated towards critical/self-reflected knowledge, knowledge that arises out of self-knowing. This provides the conditions for the emancipation of the learner, to be able to critically follow their own interests, the empowering 'of' the students. Likewise, the teacher is emancipated from being the ultimate source of all knowledge and is able to engage with the students as another learner.

However, as has been mentioned earlier, the personalisation of classroom culture can potentially conflict with the expectations of school culture when school rules are modified, or ignored, in the light of the teachers' own values and beliefs. When this is viewed from the perspective of power it suggests that the teacher with expertise can achieve a position of being an approved maverick to the extent that their individuality, their idiosyncrasies and inconsistencies are sanctioned on the basis of their overall efficacy as a teacher. The empowerment and approval of teacher expertise operates within the context of the power that is exercised by leadership within the school and especially the headteacher. This is particularly the case when determining the extent to which consistent practices are expected and reinforced. Eleanor commented on the extent to which inconsistencies can be tolerated. She described the power structure in her school as a pyramid with senior leaders establishing and developing the ethos from the top and that this included a requirement for consistent practices across the school.

ELEANOR: *I feel constrained by the power structure but not in a negative way. Alan (the headteacher) is after consistency and he wants us all to teach on the TEEP model* (the Teacher Enhancement Effectiveness Programme). *I do my own thing anyway but it is based on TEEP. This is by coincidence but it is what Alan wants. The consistency bit works positively when everybody is going in the same direction.*

Eleanor thought that when everybody is broadly going in the same direction it is possible to tolerate some variation and that there can be some flexibility within the overall constraints. She felt that headteachers need to trust teachers *to do things right*. However, she qualified this by saying that the ability of teachers in a school was mixed and that the problems faced by weaker teachers could cause problems for the whole staff.

Deciding how to respond to variations in the quality and experience of teachers is a dilemma that was raised by William (the headteacher of The Shakespeare Community School) when he was talking about the ways in which he builds relationships with staff though distributed leadership.

WILLIAM: *... so basically we let people get on with the job. We're not at all bureaucratic, so we don't say you must plan lessons in this format, we don't say we want to see your lesson plans, we are very kind of laissez-faire in that respect. We don't tell them how to run their departments but we look at the results. So we provide a* *framework, we provide the support and we are rigorous on the outcomes. Now that fits with the national strategy in terms of literacy and numeracy, getting everybody at the same level and to go beyond that you need to release people's creativity. I think that what we have slightly lost sight of (over) the past few years is that it is OK for certain staff who have been in the culture for a long time, but actually you have got a lot of new blood that is coming in all the time. And what's happening is those people come in and we have perceived that we have come too loose. And there has become too much variation in people's practice and therefore part of the (schools) teaching and learning strategy is to pull people back towards a common baseline and then to release them again.*

This statement implies that the empowerment of teachers to have greater freedom and autonomy is something that can only be granted after a period of time when they have proved themselves in terms of the outputs of their teaching. The power exercised by headteachers that allows teachers to have a greater degree of autonomy was noted and appreciated by many of the participants.

RICHARD: *I feel supported by the school and especially by the head; he believes in the Arts and believes in the subject and the life skills and social skills that it develops.*

HELEN: (The head) *has given me tremendous power, influenced the way that I teacher and given me the confidence to try new things. I feel I have been empowered and have been able to have an influence over other teachers.*

Nevertheless it was the external power of the system, as experienced by the influence of government policy and the impact of Ofsted that had the most significant impact on schools. William (headteacher of the Shakespeare Community School) expressed it this way:

WILLIAM: *There was a period about five years ago when … there was a flowering of interest in things like the Royal Society of Arts 'Opening Minds' project, things like Building Learning Power … and there were lots of schools that were starting to dismantle their regular key stage three curriculum, different time blocks, integrated humanities … There was a great flurry of interest in all of that and what I sense with the coalition government is that all of that is shutting down again and we are going back to a much more compartmentalised academic, exam focussed curriculum and a kind of … there's a lot of panic in schools. There is a desperation around results … a desperation to do whatever you can to gain that extra few per cent because the consequences of slipping through the net is the rulebook will be on your head. That's what I would say is happening.*

These pressures were also being felt by the teachers in the school, particularly those teaching subjects such as drama that are not included in lists of 'approved' subjects. There was a real sense of anger at these decisions; one teacher expressed it to me as being '*f***ing infuriating*'. The impact of the policy changes was felt to be *unprecedented*, and the pedagogical implications of the changes were felt to be *'inspired by pseudo-political values'* especially when determining that certain curriculum areas were deemed to be less academically rigorous and hence less worthwhile.

Another aspect of the external power that had an impact on teachers was the power of parents, with the power exercised by parents being particularly strong where schools were situated in, and serving, middle-class communities. One teacher pointed out that the impact of parent power on certain teachers was not to be ignored or underestimated and likened to a kind of bullying. The teacher in question said that they were *'lucky to have avoided this'*.

The social construction of the improvising teacher

How does the ecology of the school, as expressed through structure, culture and power contribute to the social construction of the improvising teacher? The improvising teacher as an expression of advanced professional practice is arrived at through a process of empowerment in which they are permitted a degree of professional autonomy and agency. This can be theorised as a three-stage process that consists of an establishment phase, a developmental phase and an improvisatory phase.

The initial establishment phase is concerned with meeting the cultural expectations of the school and conforming to professional expectations through working within defined structures.

The developmental phase is arrived at when the teacher establishes their efficacy in relation to the frames of reference provided by the school. Evidence in achieving this phase is seen in the development of confidence, experience and tacit knowledge. Teachers are able to sense 'the right thing to do' when professional decisions need to be made. This phase confers a degree of empowerment in which teachers are entrusted to 'get on with the job' in their own way.

This merges into a third phase characterised by artful improvisatory practice whereby teachers are licensed to operate within their own frame of reference, within their own lifeworld. They are acknowledged as experts due to being able to achieve results that other teachers may not be capable of achieving. In the improvisatory phase the expertise of teachers is demonstrated through improvisational practice that takes place within the personalised lifeworld of the classroom. The empowerment of their practice, supported by the leadership of the school, results in them having increased agency. This increased agency may result in them using approaches that fall outside of the expectations that apply to most other member so of staff. Consequently teachers within this phase can be seen as 'sanctioned mavericks' supported by the evidence of outcomes in terms of examination results and for their relationships with students.

This process is shown in Figure 8.2.

110 *The empirical research*

Improvisatory phase: teacher expertise demonstrated through improvisational practice and establishment of personalized 'lifeworld' of the classroom. Increased agency sanctioned through empowerment of practice. Some approaches fall outside of the expectations for most staff. 'Maverick' practice sanctioned on evidence of outcomes (exam results and human).

Developmental phase: teacher efficacy established, building of confidence, experience and tacit knowledge.

Establishment phase: expectations from leadership for conformity to professional and cultural expectations of school.

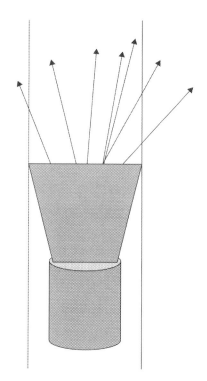

Figure 8.2 The improvising teacher: three phases of empowerment

This model outlines the phased process of negotiated cultural change which leads to the mature expression of teacher expertise characterised by improvisatory practice. This process can be summarised in the second postulate of this study, which is:

> That the improvisational nature of teacher expertise is viewed as the negotiation of a situated culture, operating as a form of empowerment linked to the created state of social agency.

Chapter summary

This chapter has provided an overview of the findings of the empirical research and presented them as theoretical frameworks. These frameworks serve to offer conceptual insights into the improvising teacher from a range of different perspectives. Theory is being used as a tool (Thomas, 2011) by which the findings of the comparative case studies can be explained, links can be made between ideas and connections made with the findings of others.

A central framework for this book is the grounded theory of advanced professional practice, which outlines the nature of teacher expertise and demonstrates the fundamental importance of improvisational practice for teachers with expertise. This framework outlines the skills and aptitudes that lie behind the concept of the improvising teacher. Acquiring this form of advanced professional practice is informed by experience, expertise and artful improvisation. One of the key assumptions that inform this study is that advanced professional practice and expertise is socially constructed. The context for professional development is looked at from an organisational perspective attending to the ways in which the teachers in the study view the concepts of structure, culture and power. This leads to a framework that outlines the process which leads to the empowering of the improvising teacher.

This brings to a conclusion Part II of the book that has presented the findings of the empirical research. In Part III, the findings and conclusions of the research are subjected to critical evaluation within an international context in order to outline a theoretical model that addresses the long-term professional development of teachers.

PART III
Implications for practice

9 Towards a long-term framework for the professional development of the improvising teacher

Introduction

The central argument of this book is that improvisation is a fundamental aspect of teaching and that the concept of the improvising teacher provides a prototype model of advanced professional practice. The tenet that emerges from the research, and which is at the heart of the grounded theory of teacher expertise, is that the development of expertise is a journey and not an end state. The development of expertise is the consequence of an ongoing adaptive process that is based on continual reflection and the improvement of practice. This process occurs over long periods of time as the accumulation of experience and expertise provides the basis for an informed understanding of artful improvisational practice. Consequently, there is a need to view professional development towards expertise as a long-term project. Drawing on literature, the research findings and the author's professional experience, this chapter addresses three issues that are pertinent to viewing professional development as a long-term process. To begin with there is the issue of what kind of professional practice and professionalism is being envisaged. Following on from this is the question of what a framework for the long-term professional development of teachers looks like. The chapter concludes by conceptualising the disposition (the mindset) and the skills that provide the foundations for an informed understanding of artful teacher improvisation.

Understanding professional practice and professionalism

The assumption about professional practice that has informed this book is that it is 'a highly specific process but one that has similarities with others involving the performance of complex and diverse skills in real time and in contexts that are unpredictable and constantly evolving' (Atkinson and Claxton, 2000: 4). The complexity of teaching arises, in part, because it is fundamentally a relational activity that is undertaken through dialogic practices that demand responding to and managing the needs of groups of students. These are the significant characteristics that make teaching a fundamentally improvisatory practice. There are also other assumptions about the nature of teaching that inform the way professional practice is conceptualised.

DOI: 10.4324/9781003223207-12

One important assumption is that teachers need to engage with higher order pedagogic practices that go beyond the transmission of knowledge and acknowledge that the goal of education is to prepare young people for their future within a dynamic and rapidly changing world. The role of the teacher is multi-faceted, and whilst there will always be a requirement for them to be engaged in the transmission of knowledge, there is also a more pertinent and challenging need for them to become facilitators of learning within a learner-centred classroom. These two modes of teaching are not mutually exclusive, and they should not be seen as a resurfacing of the debate between 'traditional' and 'progressive' teaching methods. Instead they should be conceived as being at the two ends of a continuum, which has the teacher-centred classroom at one end and a learner-centred classroom at the other.

Another factor that informs the understanding of professional practice is the issue of autonomy and the role that it plays in the encouragement of advanced practice. Barber and Mourshed (2007), for example, outline the limitations of 'top down' initiatives:

> In the end, achieving great performance in the public sector ... requires unlocking the initiative, creativity and motivation of leaders throughout the system, rather than those just at the top. This cannot be done without substantial devolution and/or providing the freedoms of a quasi-market. In short, you can mandate 'awful' to 'adequate', but you cannot mandate greatness, which must be unleashed.
>
> (Barber and Mourshed, 2007)

The implication of this argument is that teacher autonomy is essential in order to unlock initiative, creativity and motivation. However, whilst providing the profession with a mandate to develop 'greatness' is all well and good, it begs the question of what 'greatness' looks like or what constitutes 'good practice'. If the key to 'unleashing greatness' is professional autonomy, then it has to be recognised that there can be no single view of what 'good practice' might look like.

> A vibrant democracy needs an open-ended approach to 'good practice' which remains in the control of reflective and learning professionals, which remains sensitive to constantly changing local contexts, and which provides the resources to deal appropriately with the complexities involved in its identification and dissemination. In sum, the political emphasis on momentum, increasing pressure for improved performance and innovation, needs to be matched by continuity of institutions, stability for students, *professional autonomy* [my emphasis] and adequate funding.
>
> (Coffield and Edward, 2009)

An open-ended approach to 'good practice' is a reminder that notions of advanced practice necessarily have to take into account the context in which teachers work and the embedded values that underpin the culture of the shared working environment. There needs to be an acknowledgement of the situated nature of advanced practice.

Finally, there is a need to consider the epistemological foundations of professional practice and the nature of the knowledge base that informs advanced professional practice. Ryle's (1945) distinction between 'knowing that' and 'knowing how to' has informed much of the debate concerning the knowledge base of teaching. One of the problems concerning teacher expertise, identified in the research, relates to the issue of 'knowing how to'. This is problematical due to the fact that much of what teachers 'know how to do' is informed by tacit knowledge, an aspect of unconscious competence.

Ryle's distinction is developed by Shulman (1987) who articulates the knowledge base required by teachers as comprising three elements: content knowledge (or subject knowledge), pedagogical knowledge (a general understanding of pedagogical skills) and pedagogical content knowledge (a teachers' interpretation and transformation of subject-matter knowledge in the context of facilitating student learning). The latter is seen as the key to distinguishing the knowledge base of teaching given that it lies at the intersection of content and pedagogy.

A further kind of knowledge, derived in part from professional practice, is gained through what is described as critical professional learning, a process by which professional practice is related to theory and research in order to bring about a critical perspective that can inform the development of practice and (ideally) inform policy. Critical professional learning has been described as the process by which teachers come to understand their professional values, attitudes and beliefs and gain an understanding of how these impact on their conceptual understanding and their knowledge of learners and pedagogy. It also enables teachers to research and validate their practice in order to inform their development and that the rationale for practice can be clearly articulated (Mitchell, 1997). This additional form of knowledge that relies upon and extends pedagogical content knowledge also unites Ryle's distinction between 'know that' and 'knowing how to'. At the heart of critical professional learning is a symbiotic relationship between conceptual understanding and practical skills, a point that will be developed later in this chapter.

The understanding of professional practice that is being advanced in this chapter can be summarised as follows:

- teaching is a complex activity that is fundamentally relational and improvisational;
- teachers need to operate along a continuum in which the transmission of knowledge (in a teacher-centred classroom) is at one end and the facilitation of learning (in a learner-centred classroom) is at the other;
- teachers need to be able to exercise their autonomy and this is a condition of developing advanced practice;
- there is no single, essentialist view of 'good practice', recognition has to be given to the situated nature of advanced practice;

- the knowledge base of advanced practice includes, and is facilitated by, critical professional learning, which empowers teachers to become learners of and within their professional context in order to enable them to critically engage with their own practice and contribute to their school as a genuine learning organisation.

Reconceptualising professionalism: the authorised teacher

The assumptions outlined above lead to a reconceptualisation of professionalism through the professional identity of 'the authorised teacher'. This identity comprises three concepts: 'authenticity', 'authorisation' and 'authoring' and is outlined in Figure 9.1.

The three concepts of authenticity, authorisation and authoring are interrelated, and together they outline a form of professionalism and advanced professional practice that acknowledges autonomy and the warrants that permit the teacher to make professional judgements 'in the moment'. This view of professionalism values the unique and situated nature of experience and expertise and acknowledges the improvisational nature of teaching. Together these concepts comprise the 'authorised' teacher as a form of professionalism that is aligned to and underpinned by the concepts of expertise and improvisation.

Authenticity

Authenticity as a professional requirement is a quality that was noted in the research. Headteachers stated that it was extremely important that teachers were able to 'be themselves' in the classroom. They thought

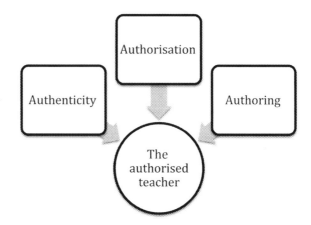

Figure 9.1 The authorised teacher

that teachers should be seen as individuals who are able to display their humanity and be perceived as 'real people' by the students. A common understanding of authenticity is of a person who is genuine and sincere, who is true to themselves, acts according to this understanding and whose opinion can therefore be accepted. Such a view is based on the assumption that the essence of a 'real self' lies at the core of our personality and that certain authentic moments occur when one is connected to one's 'true' self, to one's 'own truth' (Irvine and Reger, 2006: 5 cited in Thompson, 2016: xxiii).

Neil Thompson offers a more nuanced understanding of authenticity in his book *The Authentic Leader* (2016), and these ideas offer useful insights when applied to teaching. The perception of authenticity, which underpins Thompson's work, draws on existential philosophy. The existentialist viewpoint distinguishes between authenticity and, its opposite, bad faith:

> Sartre used the term 'bad faith' to refer to the tendency for individuals to, in effect, lie to themselves, to deny (and seek to avoid) their own freedom and their own ability to choose. The existentialist idea of authenticity encompasses the need to acknowledge that, while we are surrounded by all sorts of constraints and limitations, we are none the less free to make choices … however restricted our circumstances may be, the need to choose remains.
>
> (Thompson, 2016: xxiv)

To deny that we have choices, to create a deterministic picture of ourselves, is to act inauthentically. The improvising teacher, engaging in continual adaptation that arises from engagement in complex adaptive practice, is adept at creating alternative possibilities determined by authentic responses.

Thompson identifies other terms that play an important part in the vocabulary of authentic leadership and that can easily be applied to teaching. He starts with two related concepts: agency and ownership. Agency refers to the recognition that we can act, that we can be 'agentic beings' and not just passive victims of circumstance. This is related to the idea of ownership, the recognition that we have to take responsibility for our actions, for the choices we make and therefore the consequences of these actions. These two terms, agency and ownership, are fundamental to the idea of empowerment, of becoming stronger and more confident in the ways in which we can have more control over our lives.

A further significant concept is that of self-awareness which, for Sartre, can be understood in relation to two key concepts, facticity and transcendence. Facticity relates to the limitations placed upon us, the things we cannot change, that we have no control over, whilst transcendence refers to our capabilities to go beyond the limitations of facticity. These concepts have a particular resonance given that they are closely aligned to the understanding of improvisation that has informed this book. The existentialist notions of facticity and transcendence reflect the relationship between design structures (those fixed, non-negotiable elements) and the emergent structures (that permit agency, creativity and flexibility). The very act of improvisation can be seen as an expression, the physical manifestation and realisation of existentialist thought, and it is for this reason that notions of authenticity are at the heart of the professional conceptualisation of the authorised teacher.

To summarise, the concept of authenticity admits the possibility of agency, that we can 'act' (be agentic) and that we do not have to submit to being the passive victims of circumstance. The implications of this are that we have to take ownership for our actions and their consequences and we have to accept responsibility for what we do. This is an empowering process by which individuals can take greater control of our lives.

Authorisation

The concept of authorisation follows on from and arises out of the concept of authenticity. Through the empowerment of the self and the perceptions of being authentic, we then are in a position to empower others. Authorisation is about having the power to influence action, opinion and belief, and of having an opinion or testimony that is accepted. Authorisation can be seen as a confirmed professional identity derived from a situated community of learning. This identity acknowledges, and is derived from, the actual and potential professional knowledge that the teacher has of their own practice and about the particular educational setting of which they are a member. There is also the unique and particular self-knowledge that they have about their own unique career pathway. It is the accumulation of this knowledge and experience that provides the teacher with their professional status.

Authoring

The third concept, authoring, is concerned with the origination or 'writing' of a statement or account, the processes by which teachers 'write' or create their own professional identity within a critical framework. The 'writing' can take many forms; it is not necessarily or strictly tied to the production of a written text. Authoring is concerned with the multiplicity of ways in which teachers create, communicate and disseminate their professional status. Whilst this concerns their subject knowledge, pedagogic knowledge or pedagogic content knowledge, it also includes their values and beliefs, their knowledge of the school or context in which they work and their understanding of wider educational issues. There are many opportunities whereby teachers can engage in this professional discourse: through formal and informal interactions with other staff, parents as well as their daily interactions with their students. Post-graduate courses at masters or doctoral level provide significant, and in many ways ideal, opportunities for the authoring of professional practice. However, these are not the only opportunities through which teachers author their professional status. Engaging in communities of practice and sharing good practice and professional learning provide valuable sites for this discourse.

The interrelated nature of these three concepts now becomes apparent. The authoring of situated and personalised knowledge, when related to theory-, research- or evidence-based practice provides teachers with critical perspectives that support the authorisation of their practice. As critical professional learners who are able to articulate the rationale for their teaching, they become the authority for their own pedagogic practice. They are also in a position to share that knowledge with their peers, supported by communities of practice that are committed to the leverage of continual change by embedding and supporting professional learning. Drawing on their own experience as a professional, articulating their values and beliefs and sharing them with other teachers reinforce the authenticity of their own practices. A key principle of professional development programmes is to support teachers to articulate their personal values and beliefs and for them to see how these relate to their professional practice. Opportunities to bring personalised knowledge into the domain of professional development are important because they can counter the tendency to act in bad faith. This can arise, for example, when teachers deny themselves control of their actions and act in ways that run counter to what they believe in.

The concept of the 'authorised teacher' offers a view of professionalism that acknowledges that professional practice is derived from and informed by a broad knowledge base. This knowledge base includes 'knowing that' alongside 'knowing how' and is informed by theoretical and conceptual understanding and the tacit knowledge gained from personal experience. Above all it views teaching as a humanistic activity characterised by a dynamic and dialogic relationship between teachers and students. The personality, values and beliefs of the teacher will inform the nature of that relationship. As the basis for developing a framework of teacher development it offers an alternative pathway for the development of advanced practice that is based on self-referential activity, critical reflection and research that is moderated through interaction with other professionals within a community of practice. The authorised teacher offers a starting point and an end goal for professional development. In the next section of this chapter a long-term framework for teacher development, based on the professional values outlined above, is outlined which is designed to support the continuing professional development of authorised teachers.

A long-term model of teacher development

A framework to support the long-term professional development of teachers is something that is lacking and yet, as can be seen by the arguments advanced in this book, is a necessity in the nurturing and development of teacher expertise.

Hoban's (2002) argument that there is 'the need for a coherent theoretical framework to guide long term teacher learning and support educational change' (3) is based on a global perspective that acknowledges there is a demand for educationalists to respond to the needs and challenges of the 21st century. He notes the need for a dynamic approach to the professional development of teachers informed by the changing nature of schools as they adapt to preparing young people for a world where (to use the much quoted phrase) 'the jobs that many young people will be doing have not yet been invented'.

> If educational change is conceptualised as a complex system then short term approaches to teacher learning are inadequate .... The bottom line is that efforts for educational change need a long term approach to support teachers through the non-linear process of change requiring schools to be reconceptualised as learning environments for their teachers.
>
> (Hoban, 2002: 38–39)

Hoban argues that the literature on teachers' professional learning is inadequately theorised, and this book, in part, is a response to that argument. In the previous chapter, the development of the improvising teacher was outlined as a three-phase process involving an establishment phase, a developmental phase and an improvisatory phase. In order to be able to improvise artfully, as Quintilian would put it, there is a need for structure, skill and knowledge in the subject matter, an awareness of the means they can use and the acquisition of a repertoire.

The long-term model of teacher development that is described below informs the progression to becoming an improvising teacher by suggesting a sequential approach to building a repertoire of skills and the disposition that supports artful improvisation.

This approach has evolved from consultancy work undertaken by the author and a four-level framework (Sorensen and Coombs, 2010a) that was created prior to and separately from the research outlined in Part II of this book. This framework has been subject to revision in the light of the findings of the research and the literature on expertise, and specific attention has been given to the five-level theory of expertise proposed by Dreyfus and Dreyfus (1986).

The model, which outlines a progression from initial training to advanced professional practice (the improvising teacher), is conceived as a journey from a teacher-centred classroom to a learner-centred classroom.

However, the ability to progress from a teacher-centred classroom to a learner-centred classroom is not solely a matter of developing practical skills based around pedagogical content knowledge. Any framework that attempts to address the long-term development of teachers also needs to address the issue of metanoia, a 'shift of mind' (Senge, 2006: 13), recognising that the progression of skills and professional experience also requires a cognitive shift in the way in which teachers perceive learners. The development of a cognitive mindset therefore is a necessary accompaniment to the development of skills and competencies, one that recognises there is a symbiotic relationship between disposition and action. Drawing upon Bruner (cited in Leach and Moon, 1999: 10) the progression through the four levels is accompanied by an appropriate 'shift of mind' in the way that teachers perceive the minds of students.

This is a sequential model in that progression to the next level requires the consolidation of the competencies and skills in the previous one. The model functions as a diagnostic framework, which enables teachers to identify particular aspects of practice that they need to develop.

Table 9.1 summarises how the three phases of empowerment towards becoming an improvising teacher relate to the Dreyfus and Dreyfus (1986) five-level model of expert development, Sorensen and Coombs (2010a) four levels of teacher development and Bruner's descriptions of the ways that teachers perceive learners.

Table 9.1 Comparison of relationships between the improvising teacher, Dreyfus and Dreyfus (1986), Sorensen and Coombs (2010a) and Bruner's teacher perceptions of students.

The Improvising Teacher – Three Phases of Empowerment	Dreyfus and Dreyfus (1986) – Five Levels	Sorensen and Coombs (2010a) – Four Levels of Teacher Development	Bruner's Teacher Perceptions of Students
Establishment	L1 – novice	Level 1	Students seen as imitative learners. Students seen as learning from didactic exposure: the acquisition of propositional knowledge
	L2 – advanced beginner	Level 2	
	L3 – competent		
Developmental	L4 – proficient	Level 3	Students seen as thinkers: the development of intersubjective interchange and focus on students perspective on learning
Improvisational	L5 – expert	Level 4	Students as knowledgeable: the management of 'objective' knowledge. Teachers help students to grasp the distinction between personal knowledge and 'what is to taken to be known' by the culture

The next section looks at each of the three phases in detail identifying the key skills and the implicit mind set.

The establishment phase

The establishment phase incorporates the following:

- Levels 1 and 2 (Sorensen and Coombs, 2010a)
- Novice teacher/advanced beginner/competent teacher (Dreyfus and Dreyfus, 1986)
- Students perceived as imitative learners/students seen as learning from didactic exposure: the acquisition of propositional knowledge (Bruner)

This phase is based on achieving basic levels of competence and being able to teach an effective lesson. Whilst all teachers at the beginning of their careers can demonstrate very different levels of competence, one of the common characteristics is a primary concern for their own survival within the classroom environment. Given that it is not possible to account for the prior experiences of all teachers at the start of their teaching career, a number of generalised assumptions have been made that inform the creation of level 1 (Sorensen and Coombs, 2010a) in order to provide a baseline for future developments. These assumptions are:

- that the primary motivation of the novice teacher will be to focus on their own survival in the classroom;
- becoming a novice teacher requires the acquisition of certain basic competencies and skills;
- that the acquisition of these skills are fundamental to building positive relationships and trust with their students;
- progression as a teacher will not be possible until these basic skills have been mastered.

Based on these assumptions there is a need for teachers to acquire skills in six key areas.

1. Basic classroom management skills, including behaviour management
2. Planning a lesson
3. Creating and communicating effective learning objectives for each lesson
4. Developing strategies for starting lessons that ensure the students are engaged in learning within the first ten minutes
5. Utilising partners in learning – working with Learning Support Assistants
6. Creating an appropriate learning environment: room layout, seating plans, classroom displays that support learning, displaying and celebrating students work.

The confidence and experience that is gained through acquiring the skills in Level 1 allows attention to be given to building and developing relationships with students and to develop a knowledge base that enables the teacher to meet students' individual learning needs. The understanding that teachers gain of their students through classroom interactions is supported by data and other information gathered by the school. This wider information is then used to differentiate different learning outcomes for individuals and groups of students within each class.

Level 2 (Sorensen and Coombs, 2010a) comprises four key skills:

1. Using questions to develop thinking skills
2. Assessment for learning
3. Using data to identify individual learning needs
4. Differentiation

The developmental phase

The developmental phase incorporates the following:

- Level 3 (Sorensen and Coombs, 2010a)
- The proficient level (Dreyfus and Dreyfus, 1986)
- Students seen as thinkers: the development of inter-subjective interchange and focus on students perspective on learning (Bruner)

The developmental phase as a teacher is achieved through gaining a greater range of strategies to promote learning, broadening the repertoire of approaches for relating to students. These include active learning techniques that provide opportunities for students to become equal participants in the learning process. The choice of active learning strategies will be dependent on the subject being taught and the age range of the students. These techniques could include: role playing, case studies, group projects, think-pair-share, peer teaching, debates, just-in-time teaching and short demonstrations followed by class discussion.

Supporting this extended range of teaching strategies is the development of metacognitive approaches that enable students to gain a greater awareness of the ways in which they learn.

This phase comprises three main skill areas. Due to their broad and sophisticated nature a longer time scale is required to develop these higher level pedagogic skills. They can perhaps be more accurately described as areas of longer-term study and development.

1. Using active learning strategies and group work
2. Using 'learning to learn' strategies
3. Coaching in the classroom

The improvisational phase

The improvisational phase incorporates the following:

- Level 4 (Sorensen and Coombs, 2010a)
- The expert level (Dreyfus and Dreyfus, 1986)
- Students as knowledgeable: the management of 'objective' knowledge (Bruner)

The improvisational phase is characterised by the teacher having greater agency and being empowered to make professional decisions according to their own principles and values. This practice is accepted as being of a high professional standard by the school or setting in which the teacher operates. In line with the Dreyfus model of expertise they no longer need to rely on rules, guidelines or maxims and have an intuitive grasp of situations based on deep tacit understanding. Their practice therefore is significantly improvisational as they are able to respond intuitively and spontaneously to unexpected situations. They have an understanding of how to make the best use of the improvisational aspect of their teaching and are able to make choices as to when this is appropriate. Their artful improvisatory expertise is demonstrated through conscious use of their improvisational skills and the establishment of a personalised 'lifeworld' of the classroom. Their professional authority allows them increased agency and some of their practices may fall outside the expectations required for other members of staff. Approval for these 'sanctioned mavericks' is approved on the evidence of their efficacy as teachers as seen in their examination results and the positive relationships that they are able to engender with a wide range of students.

The skills demonstrated in the improvisational phase would include:

1. Being able to help students to grasp the distinction between personal knowledge and 'what is to taken to be known' by the culture
2. Establishing a learner-centred classroom
3. Developing an improvisation mindset and a range of techniques that support artful improvisation in their teaching
4. Teaching creatively and teaching creativity
5. Developing creativity in students
6. Teaching 'outstanding' lessons

Developing artful improvisation

The final section of this chapter looks at the improvisatory phase in greater detail giving specific attention to the ways in which teachers can be supported to engage in artful improvisation. In order to do this it seems both appropriate and essential to provide teachers with understanding, skills and knowledge about the nature and practice of improvisation in order to encourage and support their advanced practice.

The development of artful improvisation involves two dimensions: an improvisation mindset (the disposition to improvise) and the skills that support improvisatory practice. The relationship between disposition and skills is symbiotic in nature. Having a mindset to improvise encourages the development of improvisatory skills, and, similarly, the experience of improvising supports the development of an improvisation mindset.

The improvisation mindset

The improvisation mindset is informed by three attitudes or dispositions: permission, adaptation and personalisation. The first disposition of the improvisation mindset is concerned with the teacher giving themselves permission (and/or being given permission) to improvise and to develop an improvisational approach to teaching. Understanding the nature of improvisation and how it can enhance and enrich learning in the classroom supports this aspect of the mindset.

Secondly, as a consequence of giving oneself permission to improvise, there is the disposition to being open to the continual adaptation of classroom practice. Adaptation takes two forms. The first is when a lesson plan is adjusted, or even abandoned, in response to a change in the direction of learning; this could be described as adaptation IN action. A second is the adaptation of an activity or lesson after it has happened, adjusting it to meet the requirements and needs of another class or taking into account some aspects of the lesson that did not work or could be improved. This could be described as adaptation ON action. This disposition is marked by a willingness to try out different ideas.

The third disposition is concerned with personalisation, the willingness to develop a personalised approach to teaching and, where possible, the environment you are teaching in. In the same way that a jazz musician aims to develop a personal sound, the improvising teacher finds different ways to personalise their teaching. This can be seen in the personalisation of the teacher–pupil relationship: getting to know the students as individuals and by the way in which the teacher presents himself or herself as an individual.

The improvisation skill set

The skill set that characterises the improvisatory phase of teaching is based around four key practices. These improvisational practices are commonly used by actors, dancers, comedians and musicians, and they are particularly relevant to teachers. The four skills are noticing, creating dialogue, making connections and adapting.

Noticing

Noticing is one of the most important skills that improvisers can have. The ability to notice things is about seeing everything as an offer. Being able to notice what is happening provides greater potential for response. This is particularly true for the teacher in the classroom when they pick up and respond to the students' ideas and suggestions. A common difficulty that teachers face is the continuous bombardment with information, requests, questions and distractions. Their way of coping is to screen much information out. Poynton (2013) suggests that one way to develop the skill of noticing is by being selective about what we pay attention to, by focusing on one of four levels: the wider world, the immediate environment, other people and ourselves. This approach makes the act of noticing more manageable as it is very difficult to be able to take in all levels at once.

An example of how noticing informs teaching was provided by Helen, a modern language teacher. She showed me a plastic file box with cards inside to explain how she planned her lessons. *I now use a box of teaching and learning ideas so my lessons are not so structured* (in advance). *Improvisation is the next stage for me, I don't feel so constrained. Students are enjoying the lessons more and so am I.* Helen now spends more time noticing and responding to the emotional mood of the class. *I 'read' the students more, looking for peaks and troughs and then I choose an activity* (from her file box of teaching ideas) *that responds to their mood and behaviour.* So, for example, if the energy level in the classroom is low, then she would select an activity that requires them to work in small groups to create a scenario for ordering food in a restaurant. Alternatively if the class are noisy and excitable, she will choose an activity that requires them to work individually.

Developing dialogic practice

Every conversation is an entry point into improvisation. Engaging in a dialogue is an open-ended experience that has no pre-determined outcome. For each utterance there is the need to wait for a response before determining what the next utterance will be. Dialogue in the classroom is certainly improvisatory as it is never possible to know in advance what is going to be said next. Teachers with an improvisation mindset embrace this opportunity as they know that building conversations and dialogue around learning is an important way of engaging with students and incorporating their ideas. Freire (1972) refers to this as actors in intercommunication.

Dialogic teaching is derived from the theories of Bakhtin whose view of dialogism implies that there are (at least) two voices and that there is an underlying assumption of difference. Dialogic teaching assumes a more equal relationship between teacher and students, where there is the possibility for the teacher to learn from their students. In bell hooks view, the dialogic classroom offers the possibility of an engaged pedagogy where the teacher 'must genuinely value everyone's presence There must be an ongoing recognition that everyone influences the classroom dynamic, that everyone contributes. These contributions are resources' (bell hooks, 1994: 8). One of the headteachers I interviewed described this practice as *'working with rather than on students'*.

Making connections

The classroom is a complex environment. The teacher has a lesson that they have prepared; they begin by opening up a dialogue that creates a plethora of questions. Some questions may be 'on target' in that they are appropriate to the content of the lesson, whilst others may seem irrelevant, and some offer unthought of ideas and possibilities. How should the teacher respond to this situation? The improvising teacher is able to think on their feet, pick up ideas from the class and incorporate them with their lesson. They are also adept at making the lesson relevant, connecting the content to the real world and the lives of their students and bringing together two or more seemingly disparate ideas.

Adaptation

Adapting a lesson plan 'in the moment' is the practice that most teachers think of when they talk about improvisational teaching. The need to do this can come about for a number of reasons: responding to or building on the ideas given by students, reacting to time constraints, dealing with unexpected interruptions, incorporating current topical issues or news events, accepting that the class 'just don't get' what you are teaching; the list is endless. The ability to be adaptable in order to engage with your students or to be able to clarify misunderstandings in a new way is a fundamental skill.

The ability to be able to adapt the lesson as it is happening is dependent on having a broad repertoire of responses to fall back on. Over a period of time teachers gain the experience that enables them to change their lesson plan and generate a suitable alternative. This becomes second nature when teachers are able to draw upon their tacit knowledge of 'what works' and 'what could work'.

The three dispositions of the improvisation mindset and the four improvisational skills are shown in Figure 9.2.

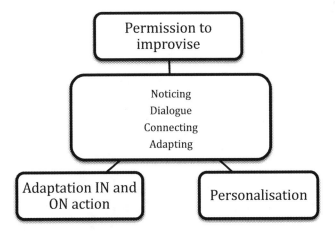

Figure 9.2 The three dispositions of the improvisation mindset and the four skills of improvisational teaching

Chapter summary

This chapter has advanced the central argument of this book that teaching involves the performance of complex and diverse skills in real time and that improvisation is a fundamental aspect of advanced professional practice. The implications of the research for practice were presented in relation to understanding the long-term process of teacher development.

The starting point for this process of teacher development has to acknowledge an appropriate conception of professionalism. The concept of the authorised teacher has been outlined as a professional identity that is congruent with the idea of the improvising teacher. Such an identity acknowledges the importance of agency and autonomy in educational decision-making and practice.

A long-term model for teacher development is described that is aligned with the three-phase empowerment of the improvising teacher. This model identifies a repertoire that the improvising teacher can draw upon and concludes with an outline of the improvisation mindset and skill set as a way of promoting artful improvisation in the classroom.

10 Afterword

The improvising teacher in the COVID-19 present

Introduction

The final draft of this book was started in April 2020 as the UK, along with other countries throughout the world, went into lockdown. Whilst the research and thinking that informs the writing took place well before the COVID-19 pandemic, the response of teachers during this unprecedented emergency brought their resilience, professional capabilities and expertise to the fore and highlighted the significance of their improvisational ability. It was as if on a daily basis we were being reminded of the importance and the value of being an improvising teacher.

This chapter considers the global impact the COVID-19 pandemic has had on the education sector, where teachers have found themselves to be at the forefront of coping and responding to the challenges caused by lockdown restrictions. The pandemic has exposed both the strengths and weaknesses of societies across the world and this has had a particular impact on educational institutions. Nurseries, schools, colleges, universities and other organisations have been forced to make local decisions within short timescales, determining what is best for the students that they serve. In short the global emergency has challenged all teachers and educational leaders to draw upon their improvisatory skills, having to make professional judgements within a policy vacuum characterised by inadequate or non-existent government guidelines. The decisions and actions that teachers have had to make highlight the importance of improvisation, especially when faced with circumstances where the usual and predicted courses of action are no longer appropriate.

International reports from the United Nations (2020), the International Commission on the Futures of Education (ICFE, 2020) and Brink et al. (2020) outline the stark reality of the impact that COVID-19 has already had on the education of young people across the world. At the same time, they note the way that the crisis has stimulated innovation within the education sector. In order to capture and record some of the ways in which teachers have responded to the challenges they have faced the author undertook a small-scale study, gathering narratives from teachers across the

DOI: 10.4324/9781003223207-13

world. The narratives provide a unique case study of improvising teachers working in a range of different contexts and different countries. This data is supplemented by similar research, a study undertaken with teachers in France and Italy (Mincu and Granata, 2021), that explores how the education emergency represented an opportunity for some teachers to explore innovative equitable approaches that differed from their actual practices and pedagogical cultures.

The chapter concludes by outlining the lessons that have already been learnt from the COVID-19 pandemic and the implications these have for education in general and the role of teachers in the future.

> For a number of reasons, we cannot return to the world as it was before. As we 'build back resilient (sic)', we need to ensure that education systems are more flexible, equitable and inclusive.
>
> (United Nations, 2020: 23)

This sends out a clear message that there is a need to acknowledge the autonomy and professional judgement of teachers and that the ability to improvise is something to be valued and supported.

COVID-19: the context

The United Nations Policy Brief *Education during COVID-19 and beyond* (United Nations, 2020) provides a stark overview of the impact of the COVID-19 pandemic, which has created the largest disruption of education systems in history. To date it has affected nearly 1.6 billion learners in more than 190 countries and all continents. Closures of schools and other learning spaces have impacted 94% of the world's student population and this has been up to 99% in low and lower-middle income countries. The crisis is exacerbating pre-existing education disparities, exposing the gap between the most and the least well off. Students with disabilities are facing barriers due to the absence of necessary equipment, internet access, accessible materials and support that would allow them to follow online programmes (United Nations, 2020). The report goes on to state that learning losses also threaten to extend beyond this generation, erasing decades of progress, not least the progress that has been made in supporting girls and young women's access to education and maintaining retention.

Furthermore there have been substantial effects beyond education. The closure of schools and other educational institutions has hampered the provision of essential services to children and communities including access to nutritious foods, the ability of parents to work and the increased risk of violence to women and girls.

From the outset of the pandemic, teachers were immediately tasked with implementing distance learning modalities, often without sufficient guidance, training or resources within short timescales. Yet in spite of these pressures the report notes that the crisis has stimulated an extraordinary amount of innovation within the education sector. This response is a reminder of the crucial role that teachers play as key workers, alongside doctors, nurses, other health service workers and those responsible for the distribution of food and other essential services. An analysis of the international reports identifies six areas where teachers have made creative and innovative contributions during the pandemic:

1. innovations in distance learning;
2. addressing poverty and inequality;
3. supporting students with special educational needs;
4. creating new learning spaces;
5. assessing and examining students' progress;
6. maintaining relationships: supporting the social aspects of learning.

The next section of this chapter will look at each of these six themes using narratives of teachers from across the world taken from a small-scale case study. These examples illustrate their improvisatory responses to situations that they have not encountered before, situations that have tested their ability to 'know what to do when you don't know what to do' (Claxton, 1999).

Requests were made through social media to teachers in all phases of education to share their stories about the ways that they have improvised during the pandemic. The teachers that responded were sent further information about the research, a consent form and a questionnaire. Respondents were also offered the option of an online interview. Six respondents were willing to provide their narratives. Some of the respondents have chosen for their names to be anonymised whilst others have requested that their contributions are attributable to them.

Innovations in distance learning

The immediate task that faced teachers when lockdown procedures were introduced was to implement distance learning. Home learning and on-line teaching created many challenges requiring all teachers to develop a whole new skill set in terms of developing proficiency in on-line teaching. The pandemic has exposed the inequalities in technological provision in many homes with examples of three or four children in one family having to share one mobile phone. In addition to creating on-line content for all lessons alternative provision was also required to support learning in the home that did not require computers. The unique authority and significance of the teacher came to the fore and in many instances they played a key role in communicating with and supporting local communities.

Asher teaches art, philosophy and college writing at the School of Arts and Sciences at St. George's University in Grenada, West Indies. One of the key innovations that he made when all teaching went online was to make everything abundantly visual.

ASHER: I had used audio/visuals in in-person classes before but once we went online, I started using our education platform, Sakai,[1] as a place to do lesson planning and archiving so the students could always go back for resources. I created visual syllabi in Canva[2] so students could check for important dates etc. at a glance. I created additional content, i.e. short videos, that supplemented the time spent in Zoom. I also utilised platforms such as Nearpod[3] to do interactive/collaborative lessons, which was particularly effective when I was assessing writing in real time. I got my students to use Flipgrid[4] in order to give short visual presentations which is a good way to get to know them better and more engaging than sharing drawings, for example, in a discussion board.

Additionally, besides making things visual and providing more ways to collaborate, I have tried to consider elements that enhance the Zoom sessions themselves. I create Zoom backgrounds that are thematic and include important dates like upcoming deadlines, etc. I also play instrumental music at the beginning of class and while students may be working on something in class.

NS: What impact did this have on your students?

ASHER: I believe my students are more engaged based on the feedback I've received. Class sessions vary slightly depending on the subject and what we are working on and so students can't expect to come to class and listen passively.

NS: In your opinion how important is it that teachers incorporate improvisation into their practice?

ASHER: I believe it is vital, particularly with online and blended learning environments. For example, as I would work on my Nearpod presentations, I would have a backup version that I could present on Google Slides if Nearpod crashed, which it did at times.

Mincu and Granata's (2021) small-scale case study of teachers in France and Italy viewed the improvisatory abilities of teachers through the lens of 'teacher leadership': 'the process by which teachers, individually and collectively, influence their colleagues, principals, and other members of school communities to improve teaching and learning practices with the aim of increased student learning and achievement' (York-Barr and Duke, 2004: 287–288 cited in Mincu and Granata, 2021: 2). The French/Italian context was chosen on account of the similarities in the two systems being more important that the divergences. Both countries are characterised by having flat horizontal school structures in which school leadership is relatively weak and teacher autonomy is strong, as in determining course content.

Most of the teachers interviewed by Mincu and Granata reported having acted autonomously when devising distance learning. Few teachers collaborated prior to lockdown but the emergency situation forced greater cooperation, with teachers becoming more confident in sharing ideas with colleagues. They also commented that they had received little support and guidance from their headteachers who were unaware of the great work they done during lockdown. There was a fear that some of the most innovative teaching initiatives might have provoked a negative reaction:

> The headteacher did not hinder me, but because he was not aware of what I was doing. Over the years I have learned to do this. The most innovative actions are not understood and sometimes even frowned upon. In the past, some of my initiatives have provoked negative reactions.
> (IT, HS4l) (Mincu and Granata, 2021: 11)

Addressing poverty and inequality

The teachers' role in communicating with their local community has been especially significant when coping with the inequalities that have been exposed during lockdown. The pandemic has had the hardest impact on the poorest families, especially those families with young children. The *Learning Through Disruption* research project ran from May to August 2021 and set out to identify how a small sample of primary schools in the UK had been dealing with the varied impacts of COVID over the course of the pandemic and what knowledge had been accrued to contribute to rebuilding a more resilient and more equal education system (Moss et al., 2021). The report identifies multiple ways in which families were turning to schools and where teachers were engaged in providing additional support for both children and their families. In the early stages of the pandemic the most immediate priority was making sure that children were fed and in some case this meant teachers were distributing food directly from the school to the door. Teachers became even more aware of the deprivations faced by families living in property and became a vital lifeline. Already aware of the high level of deprivation teachers worked to provide clothes, shoes, toiletries and sanitary products. As one headteacher commented

> We are much more aware of [family poverty] now because during the pandemic we've had to signpost families to food banks, we've had to take packs of learning to certain families because they don't have internet access at home, they don't have computers [...] the pandemic has first of all enabled us to know our community in different ways, in more meaningful ways and probably more accurate ways.
> (Moss et al., 2021: 9)

The process of delivering food and learning resources provided teachers with an opportunity to maintain contact with and support those children living in vulnerable places. As the report states 'Schools are picking up the pieces from a welfare and social services system that no longer provides a real safety net for families. For those schools, the impacts of poverty on children's lives are impossible to ignore' (Moss et al., 2021: 9).

Juggling the additional necessary roles of 'social worker' and 'mental health nurse' has brought considerable stress on many teachers and their well-being became a priority for headteachers and school leaders. Mincu and Granata (2021) report that some of the teachers in France and Italy went far beyond their strictly didactic tasks, taking care of the mental health of their students. One of the teachers commented that:

> I was worried about them and it wasn't easy to relate from a distance. […] I immediately tried to get out of my role as a subject teacher and help them to cope and interpret the situation they were living. It appeared as my main work. […] I tried to make them express, speak and write in order not to keep their questions and concerns for themselves. […] I felt responsible for their mental health. (IT HS4)
>
> (Mincu and Granata, 2021: 11)

Supporting students with special educational needs

For some students with special educational needs home schooling is not a possibility. In these circumstances the students have continued to attend their schools but the teachers have had to work within particular restrictions to ensure their own safety and the safety of others.

'Sebastian' works in a Special School in Wales teaching children and young people diagnosed with autism across both Primary and Secondary phases. He has worked as a teacher for 25 years and works with a primary phase class of children aged between four and ten years old (two female and six male) all of whom have been diagnosed with autism and most have significant learning needs particularly with regard to verbal communication, limited motor skills and the ability to cooperate with others. The interview he gave provides insights into the particular challenges faced by those teaching students with special educational needs.

SEBASTIAN: When the COVID-19 Pandemic first hit the country and we were directed to work from home in March 2020 all teaching staff were forced to improvise whether they were aware of it or not! I led a team of three Teaching Assistants (TAs) who would focus on developing particular skills on a one-to-one basis using art and craft skills, numeracy games, 'Bucket'[5] and sensory activities to engage with and explore materials and develop focus, concentration and attention. On a week-to-week basis I'd develop a loose 'plan' based on an evaluation of individual progress and development by agreeing the week's aims and strategies with the Teaching Assistants.

During lockdown an obvious priority was to establish contact with learners and carers at the earliest opportunity. The school uses an online platform called Class Dojo[6] and this came into its own when the classes were learning at home. I used it to suggest tailored activities for learners that incorporated elements of our morning routines and rituals; I read and posted stories so they could hear my voice and shared work done by the learners with their carers at home. This platform allowed us to communicate discretely with parents and carers to encourage, facilitate and interact with families at home.

NS: What impact did this have?

SEBASTIAN: I would say that for those parents and carers who engaged fully with the Class Dojo activities and shared stories and routines with the learners and posted outcomes, the evidence suggested that learners responded positively. Parents in particular began to realise how they could work with their child at home and enjoy the process of learning together. One parent in particular became so enthusiastic about the effects of 'Bucket' that she used it every day – with her other children as well as the learner in class! Parents and carers shared walks, sensory exploration, developed arts and crafts skills and were enthusiastic about listening to stories from the teachers and teaching assistants they recognised. Parents and carers were contacted by telephone regularly to gain feedback to improve the quality of the experience. I found it very useful to be working in a closer partnership with families, helping to give them more confidence to engage in learning activities with their children. In some cases this led to parents and carers growing closer and learning more about their child's needs and abilities.

NS: In your opinion how important is it that teachers incorporate improvisation into their practice?

SEBASTIAN: It is essential when you are working with learners who manifest diverse additional learning needs; I do it every day in the classroom. Rituals and routines are important to reassure and allow participation by learners. Check-in and schedules are used to structure the day and embed expectations in the learners. Within that framework, you have to build in surprise and novelty to engage the children.

We use stories as the basis for creating small dramas and making props: I remember vividly one learner surprising us all by working independently on creating a mask of the dog from 'Room on the Broom' by Julia Donaldson. He had never before shown any engagement with using coloured pens to make craft, but in this case he wouldn't stop colouring and working until he had finished it to his satisfaction.

'Bucket' and sensory exercises are examples of activities that generate surprising outcomes and engage groups of learners with diverse needs and teachers need to work with learners to make mutual discoveries of what exactly they can and can't do given the right contexts.

NS: How valuable has this having the skill to improvise been during the COVID-19 pandemic?

SEBASTIAN: The challenge has been to encourage parents and carers to improvise too.

Creating new spaces for learning

The pandemic has brought about the need to rethink where learning can take place. In addition to home learning teachers have also sought out other options for safe learning environments and outdoor spaces in some places have been utilised. New ways of working in the classroom have needed to be developed in order to ensure the safety of all when students returned to school after lockdown restrictions were eased. Lori McKee, a teacher working with undergraduate students on a Bachelor of Education course in Canada, contributed the following case study.

Box 10.1

Together Apart Pathways

Dr Lori McKee, Assistant Professor, Faculty of Education
  St Francis Xavier University, Antigonish, NS, Canada.

In Spring 2020, many classrooms worldwide were shuttered to slow the spread of COVID-19. Though the pandemic continued, in Fall 2020, I returned to my university classroom in rural, eastern Canada to teach pre-service elementary teachers through a face-to-face, masked and physically distanced instructional model. This was a novel approach in Canada as many universities pivoted to online instruction (Rushowy, 2020).[7] Moreover, this was a novel approach for *me* as an educator even though I had taught in elementary schools for 20 years and had taught courses in different formats in teacher education, I had never taught under these conditions previously. It was a very challenging year as the pedagogies and classroom activities that 'worked' in the past were no longer supportive. The conditions were ripe for improvisation and innovation. In this case study I share a practice called *Together Apart Pathways* that emerged within this context.

Why this practice? What prompted the innovation?

Together Apart Pathways arose from my concern that though my students and I were in the same *physical* space (with 6 feet between seats), our class was *socially* distanced. We experienced challenges with communication and relationship building. As a result, the classroom felt uncomfortable; we were a group of masked strangers (McKee, 2020).[8] I tried to build the kinds of relational environments that are vital to supporting learning, but I was unsuccessful in many attempts. For example, when I invited students to 'turn and talk' the combination of the elevated volume required to speak across a distance and masks that muffled voices, made oral communication unintelligible. When I used online spaces to support oral conversations, we experienced audio feedback due to the echoing in our cavernous classroom. I knew I needed to create a conduit for minimizing social distance while also maintaining physical distance. I named the practice that emerged *Together Apart Pathways* because I wanted my pedagogy and its intentions to be visible to my class of pre-service teachers to show my attempts to innovate my pedagogies.

What is this practice? How does it work?

Together Apart Pathways leverages technologies including PowerPoint and Google's JamBoard (Google, 2019)[9] to invite students to connect with one another in collegial conversations. In my teacher education classes, I use PowerPoint to provide a visual aid. When it was time for *Together Apart Pathways,* the PowerPoint slide came alive through animated transitions between slides, and text boxes that spun and bounced across the screen accompanied by the playing of catchy music (I used the theme song from an old television show called 'Knight Rider'). At a point in the music, a QR code (with the embedded JamBoard link) appeared on the slide, and students used their mobile device to scan to enter the JamBoard (see Figure 10.1). The goal was to get to the JamBoard before the music ended. The classroom that had been silent, uncomfortable, and even lonely was transformed into laughter with students calling across the room as they raced to the JamBoard to add their ideas using sticky notes, text, shape, images, and colour. Once the students entered the JamBoard, they added their comments on the collaborative workspace, but punctuated this by calling across the classroom, 'Great idea on the blue sticky note' and so on.

Figure 10.1 PowerPoint slide as a gateway to JamBoard

(Continued)

> ### What can we learn from this improvisation for teaching at all levels?
>
> As I reflect on *Together Apart Pathways*, I was surprised at how this small improvisation opened a space for me and my class to learn together in this new and challenging context. When considering whether, and how, to include *Together Apart Pathways* in classrooms at different levels, it is important to recognise that the 'power' of the practice was not in animations or catchy music but rested in the pedagogical design. The pedagogies:
>
> - were visible and responsive to the students and the context;
> - positioned technologies as tools in service to the learning;
> - were emergent and adaptive; the success of this practice came amidst other pedagogical flops and failures; and
> - are generative of new improvisations as they show the dynamic nature of teaching and learning in contemporary times.
>
> I share *Together Apart Pathways* as an invitation for other teachers to improvise and design innovative and responsive pedagogies in their classrooms.

'Rita' works in a free public school in Los Angeles for children and young people aged from 4 1/2 to 14 years old. Her school offers a unique learning model: students spend three days a week home-schooling and two days a week engaged in project-based learning on-campus. On-campus and virtual support is offered to parents and carers as co-educators. Her school therefore was in a strong position to adjust to coping with the COVID-19 pandemic. Outdoor spaces were used as learning spaces prior to the lockdown but since the students have returned to the classroom these opportunities are seen as particularly valuable.

NS: How has your mindset about improvisation changed?
RITA: Just the need for children to be outdoors more – myself needing to be outdoors more.

The hen-coop is big enough for children to go and sit on a log and read in there or take a computer and work in there. They can sit outside in one of the tents that are providing shade ... anywhere they are comfortable or they can be inside. There really is a free flow in or outdoors. There are enough people outside to see what's going on. It's not like they are alone and there's certainly enough people inside to know what's going on.

I'm doing this more, I did it before but now there's more. There's a lot more playtime out on the field. We have morning recess which has been extended to a half hour, a 45 minute lunch and afternoon 30 minutes of playtime. They know that when they get a break they can focus more, they know that they will get that release. So they are willing to buckle down a bit and say 'oh I've got a break coming up so I'm good'.

Assessing and examining students' progress

The importance of assessing the progress that students have made has been highlighted during the pandemic. New approaches to teaching on-line have meant that there is a need for new forms of assessment. Learning at a distance has meant that it has become vital for teachers to keep track of the progress of their students.

COVID-19 restrictions have meant that it is no longer safe to bring students together under traditional examination conditions. The cancellation of examinations in England has meant that other means of making judgements on student attainment have been attempted. The use of algorithms to determine the allocation of final grades in England in 2020 proved to be controversial. In 2021 the emphasis was placed on teacher assessment and moderation. There is evidence of grade inflation although this might be due to the fact that students have benefitted from studying at home. Teachers are 'not sure what the rules are any more'

ASHER: There are also many variables that affect students when they are learning from home and this includes having the ability to complete assignments in a timely manner. I think this is a good time to remember, as a teacher, it is important to help them navigate and learn in the process as opposed to 'punishing' them for not complying with due dates.

Between the willingness to improvise/innovate, having some grace for the students in the process, and being quick to admit if something isn't working, I think the ability to adapt has been extremely valuable.

Maintaining relationships: supporting the social aspects of learning

The demands of teaching and learning on-line have highlighted the importance of learning as a collective experience. There is an advantage to being in the room together with other students. Teachers have reported that with on-line teaching it is very difficult to judge the relationship with the student to understand how they are and how they are reacting to the lesson. So much information is lost without face-to-face contact.

The social dimension is an important part of the learning experience. Teachers have needed to find ways of promoting social interaction alongside the process of individual learning. Maintaining and building social relationships was one of the main challenges that faced 'Lowenna', the Provost and Professor of Education at a university in the South West of England. She is responsible for teaching, student and staff support on campus including the delivery of an

MA in Education. All of the students are educational practitioners of some sort, predominantly schoolteachers. A key priority for Lowenna is that students feel they belong to a professional learning community.

LOWENNA: When the pandemic hit and we knew we would have to deliver remotely the first change in my practice, my first improvisation really, was 'how do we do this and maintain a connectedness with our students?' Because the values that run through all of our provision is that we want all of our students to feel that they are part of a professional academic learning community. They are teachers in their schools but they are also academics engaged in an academic programme so that they will get a skill set that they can utilise back in their school or wherever, that will improve outcomes for pupils, teachers, schools whatever.

NS: How did you go about creating an authentic learning experience using online platforms that allowed breakout sessions as well as whole group teaching?

LOWENNA: When we started we didn't have breakout rooms so we knew that it would have to be whole group sessions and if there were going to be breakout groups then we would have to use another platform to support that. We had already worked extensively with WhatsApp with the students. The professional learning community part was that the students created a WhatsApp group and they invited us to join it so that any conversations that they wanted to have to address issues on the programme they would use that. The year 2s were already using that really effectively.

The other thing I had to consider was that the students used campus for private study, meeting up and I would encourage them to get together on their own, to study together, write assignments and share resources. This was just not going to be possible because the lockdown meant they had no access to campus. I worked out another way of doing that, so there was a quick improvisation of trying to create an online study space for them that was their own – they could bring us into this if they wanted to but if they wanted to have a space where they could have a good moan then it would be a safe space to do that.

The importance of the social aspect of learning was recognised within the study undertaken by Mincu and Granata. Some of the Italian teachers were concerned about the loneliness of foreign children because many of them had no social networks. In response to this 'they invented moments of socialisation and dialogic exchanges on their personal lives' (Mincu and Granata, 2021: 12). They found the opportunities for dialogical debate to overcome the 'very dry distance learning':

> One hour a week, on Fridays, we met to discuss together and talk about a topic. They ranged from light themes to more profound ones. Also

based on what emerged during the week ... [...] It was a completely free initiative, without obligation and obviously without any evaluation. The children who joined with enthusiasm loved it! We remembered for a moment that we are not just a teacher and pupils, but people.

(ITPS2) (Mincu and Granata, 2021: 12)

Conclusion

In what ways have ideas about improvisation changed as a consequence of the COVID-19 pandemic? And how should knowledge this inform future developments in education?

Rita stated that having the ability to improvise was invaluable as it gave her a sense of autonomy that she considered was crucial to her well-being:

RITA: Rather than being rigid ... I mean when you think about being rigid you are taking away the autonomy of children and so as an autonomous adult - I have a lot of autonomy as an educator at Da Vinci, I have to say that, I have a lot of autonomy - it feels right to be flexible. It's not going against our selves, our true selves. And it is work, I don't want people to think that it's easy ... its not easy by any means however it is quite fulfilling when you see children thriving with their autonomy. There's no push back on ... power differentials ... there you go!

Asher felt he had benefitted from having the willingness to improvise and innovate, 'having some grace for the students in the process, and being quick to admit if something isn't working, I think the ability to adapt has been extremely valuable'.

Sebastian has learnt to take more risks in the classroom

SEBASTIAN: ... especially with small groups of diverse learners. I have been tasked to work with many classes within the school, sometimes at short notice. For example, having returned to working in the classroom in 2021 I was introduced to a secondary phase class whose teacher had prepared a lesson on measuring liquids. I had not met the class before. I was presented with many bits of equipment and had three teaching assistants available. I had no plan and none was forthcoming.

I relaxed and began to improvise. Picking up a measuring cylinder I asked, 'Can any one show me what to do with this?' 'You put water in it'. 'Can you show me?' The learner went to the tap and filled the cylinder. 'There'. 'I wonder how many of those will be needed to fill that bowl over there - white boards - write your guess down. Now, you all have a bowl, fill your cylinders and see how many you need to fill your bowls!' By the end of the lesson I had engaged with each learner, set more 'research' tasks and delivered a successful and memorable lesson for these learners that I had never met before.

Mincu and Granata report that the teachers they interviewed have accepted a new reality in which there is no alternative to innovation, it has now become an obligation for everyone (Mincu and Granata, 2021: 12).

The *Learning Through Disruption* report makes the point that

> the best evidence for what should happen next remains largely at the front line, where events unfolded. That is to say, both amongst staff who have grappled with difficult problems throughout the pandemic and found ways to adapt their offer as the pandemic has gone on, and with parents who grappled with the difficult task of educating children at home.
>
> (Moss et al., 2021: 5)

Headteachers and teachers have played a crucial role in managing this crisis, taking fast action in response to novel demands and often in the face of unhelpful government guidance. The priorities for recovery are concerned with re-establishing routines, rebuilding the social skills required to learn well in large groups and helping students to remake friendships. Interestingly some teachers are acknowledging the importance of improvisational drama as a way to assist the return to the classroom. One teacher spoke of observing that many children were struggling with improvisation, imaginative play and, more generally, socializing with other children, and has been supporting this need with drama work:

> [if] they have not been doing any drama or imaginative play at home [...] there was a real lack of understanding of what that meant, to be another character, and to take that on. I think for us, in a sense, it's these younger children.
>
> (Staff S2) (Moss et al., 2021: 16)

The extraordinary resourcefulness, creativity and resilience of teachers, as they have responded to the COVID-19 pandemic, highlights the significance of improvisation and the value of professional autonomy. There is a broad consensus that as nations across the world recover from this emergency there are lessons to be learnt and that there should not be a return to the practices of the past. This is an ideal time for the profession to be given the opportunity to lead discussions that will inform policy decisions. Hopefully these discussions will reflect the arguments presented in this book: that teaching, at its best, is a fundamentally an improvisatory practice practiced by professionals who have autonomy and the agency to respond creatively within the circumstances in which they teach. In doing so it moves towards a future in which the improvising teacher is valued as a key aspect of a vibrant and dynamic educational ecology, one that sustains learning, promotes resilience and creativity and nurtures the professional development of expertise.

Notes

1. https://www.sakailms.org/
2. https://www.canva.com/education/
3. https://nearpod.com/
4. https://info.flipgrid.com/
5. Bucket is a technique from Attention Autism, which is an intervention model designed by Gina Davies. The teacher places an object/s in a bucket and sings 'I have something in my bucket, in my bucket, in my bucket, I have something in my bucket, I wonder what it is'. The activity creates a focus and supports attention building and interactive learning.
6. https://classdojo.com/
7. Rushowy, K. (2020, May 4). Colleges and universities quietly preparing to take all classes online this Fall amid COVID-19. *Toronto Star*. Retrieved from: https://www.thestar.com/politics/provincial/2020/04/28/colleges-and-universities-quietly-preparing-to-take-all-classes-online-this-fall-amid-covid-19.html?rf
8. McKee, L. (2020). Learning to teach in COVID-19. [vignette]. In M.K. Barbour, R. LeBonte, & J. Nagle, *Stories from the Field: Voices of K-12 Stakeholders During Pandemic*. Retrieved from https://drive.google.com/file/d/1FHPuErfKtPQo02nxu8crdAN-spfSb2NK/view
9. Google (2019). *Jamboard*. [software version 0.2]. Retrieved from https://chrome.google.com/webstore/detail/jamboard/ihacalceahhliihnhclmjjghadnhhnoc

References

Adams, P. (2014) *Policy and Education*, Abingdon: Routledge.
Arthur, J., Waring, M., Coe, R. and Hedges, L.V. (2012) *Research Methods and Methodologies in Education*, London: Sage.
Atkinson, T. and Claxton, G. (2000) *The Intuitive Practitioner: On the Value of Not Always Knowing What One Is Doing*, Maidenhead: Open University Press.
Auguste, B., Kihn, P. and Miller, M. (2010) *Closing the Talent Gap: Attracting and Retaining Top-Third Graduates to a Career in Teaching*. McKinsey and Company. Available at https://www.mckinsey.com/industries/education/our-insights/closing-the-teaching-talent-gap
Ball, S. (2003) 'The teacher's soul and the terrors of performativity', *Journal of Education Policy* 18 (2), 215–228.
Barber, M. and Mourshed, M. (2007) *How the World's Best School Systems Stay on Top*, McKinsey and Company. Available at https://www.mckinsey.com/~/media/mckinsey/industries/public and social sector/our insights/how the world's best performing school systems come out on top [Accessed 26 April 2021].
Barnes, J. (2001) *Early Greek Philosophers*, 2nd ed., London: Penguin.
Beck, J. (2008) 'Governmental professionalism: re-professionalising or de-professionalising teachers in England?', *British Journal of Educational Studies*, 56, 119–143. Available at https://doi.org/10.1111/j.1467-8527.2008.00401.x
Benner, P. (1984) *From Novice to Expert: Excellence and Power in Clinical Nursing Practice*, Menlo Park, CA: Addison Wesley.
Berger, P.L. and Luckmann, T. (1966) *The Social Construction of Reality*, New York: Anchor Books.
Best, S. and Kellner, D. (1991) *Postmodern Theory: Critical Interrogations*, New York: The Guildford Press.
Bolman, L.G. and Deal, T.E. (1997) *Reframing Organisations: Artistry, Choice and Leadership*, 2nd ed., San Francisco: Jossey Bass.
Braidotti, R. (2013) *The Posthuman*, Cambridge: Polity Press.
Brink, R., Ozolins, K. and Jenaus, E. (2020) Report 1: How have schools coped with COVID-19? Available at https://home.edurio.com/covid-19-impact-report1 [Accessed 22 November 2021].
British Educational Research Association (2018) *Ethical Guidelines for Educational Research*, 4th ed., London. Available at https://www.bera.ac.uk/publication/ethical-guidelines-for-educational-research-2018.
Brown, S. and McIntyre, D. (1993) *Making Sense of Teaching*, Buckingham: Open University Press.

References

Bullock, A., Stallybrass, O. and Trombley, S. (1988) *The Fontana Dictionary of Modern Thought*, 2nd ed., London: Fontana.
Burr, V. (2003) *Social Constructionism*, London: Routledge.
Burton, D. and Goodman, R. (2011) 'The masters in teaching and learning: a revolution in teacher learning or a bright light quickly extinguished?', *Journal of Education for Teaching*, 37(1), 51–61.
Callaghan, J. (1976) 'Ruskin college speech', Available at http://www.educationengland.org.uk/documents/speeches/1976ruskin.html [Accessed 21 April 2012].
Campbell, J., Kyriakides, L., Muijs, D. and Robinson, W. (2004) *Assessing Teacher Effectiveness: Developing a Differentiated Model*, Abingdon, UK: RoutledgeFalmer.
Capra, F. (1996) *The Web of Life*, London: Flamingo.
Capra, F. (1997) *Creativity and Leadership in Learning Communities*, California: Centre for Ecoliteracy.
Capra, F. (2002) *The Hidden Connections*, London: Flamingo.
Chandler, Daniel (1994) Semiotics for Beginners, [e-book type] Available at http://www.aber.ac.uk/media/Documents/S4B/ [Accessed 15 February 2012].
Charmaz, K. (2006) *Constructing Grounded Theory: A Practical Guide through Qualitative Analysis*, London: Sage.
Chase, W.G. and Simon, H.A. (1973) 'Perception in chess', *Cognitive Psychology*, 4, 55–81.
Claxton, G. (1999) *Wise Up: the Challenge of Lifelong Learning*, London: Bloomsbury.
Claxton, G. (2002) *Building Learning Power*, Bristol: TLO Limited.
Clough, P. and Nutbrown, C. (2012) *A Students Guide to Methodology*, 3rd ed., London: Sage.
Coffield, F. and Edward, S. (2009) 'Rolling out 'good', 'best' and 'excellent' practice. What next? Perfect practice?', *British Educational Research Journal*, 35(3), 371–390.
Cohen, L., Manion, L. and Morrison, K. (2011) *Research Methods in Education*, 7th ed. Abingdon: Routledge.
Collins, H. and Evans, R. (2007) *Rethinking Expertise*, Chicago: University of Chicago Press.
Conquergood, D. (2002) Performance Studies: Interventions and Radical Research1. *TDR/The Drama Review*, 46, 145–156.
Daly, C., Milton, E. and Langdon, F. (2020) 'How do ecological perspectives help understand schools as sites for teacher learning?' *Professional Development in Education*, 46 (4), 652–663, DOI: 10.1080/19415257.2020.178208
Davis, J. (2002) 'The Inner London Education Authority and the William Tyndale Junior School Affair, 1974–1976', *Oxford Review of Education*, 28 (2 & 3), 275–298.
Day, C., Kington, A., Stobart, G. and Sammons, P. (2006) 'The personal and professional selves of teachers: stable and unstable identities', *British Educational Research Journal*, 32 (4), 601–616.
Deakin Crick, R. (2006) *Learning Power in Practice: A Guide for Teachers*, London: Paul Chapman Publishing.
Deakin Crick, R., Broadfoot, P. and Claxton, G. (2004) 'Developing an effective lifelong learning inventory: the ELLI projects', *Assessment for Education*, 11 (3), 247–272.
Department for Children, Schools and Families. (2008) *Being the Best for Our Children: Releasing Talent for Teaching and Learning*, London: The Stationary Office.
Department for Children, Schools and Families. (2009) *Excellent Teacher Scheme Review*, London: DCSF.
Department for Education. (2010) *The Importance of Teaching*, London: The Stationary Office.
Department for Education. (2021) *Delivering World Class Teacher Development*, London: DfE.

Department for Education and Science. (1972) *The James Report: Teacher Education and Training*, London: HMSO.

Department for Education and Science. (1985a) *Better Schools – A Summary*, London: HMSO.

Department for Education and Science. (1985b) *Education Observed 3: Good Teachers*. A paper by HM Inspectorate, London: DES.

Dickens, C. (1854) *Hard Times*, London: Penguin Classics.

Dorsch, T.S. (1965) *Classical Literary Criticism: Aristotle, Horace, Longinus*, Harmondsworth: Penguin.

Dreyfus, S.L. and Dreyfus, H.L. (1986) *Mind Over Machine: The Power of Human Intuition and Expertise in the Age of the Computer*, New York: Simon and Schuster.

Dubin, P. (1962) *Human Relations in Administration*, Englewood Cliffs: Prentice Hall.

Durant, A (1984) *Improvisation – Arguments after the Fact' in Improvisation: History, Directions, Practice*, London: Association of Improvising Musicians.

Eagleton, T. (2008) *The Meaning of Life: A Very Short Introduction*, Oxford: Oxford University Press.

Eraut, M. (1994) *Developing Professional Knowledge and Competence*, London: The Falmer Press.

Ericsson, K.A. (2000) 'Expertise in interpreting: An expert-performance perspective', *Interpreting* 5(2), 187–220.

Ericsson, K.A., Charness, N., Feltovitch, P.J. and Hoffman, R.R. (2006) *The Cambridge Handbook of Expertise and Expert Performance*, New York: Cambridge University Press.

Evans, L. (2002) 'What is teacher development?', *Oxford Review of Education*, 28 (1), 123–137.

Evans, L. (2008) 'Professionalism, professionality and the development of education professionals', *British Journal of Educational Studies*, 56(1), 20–38.

Faulkner, P. (1977) *Modernism*, London: Methuen.

Ferre, F. (1982) *Language, Logic and God*, New York: Harper and Row.

Finlayson, J.G. (2005) *Habermas: A Very Short Introduction*, Oxford: Oxford University Press.

Fischlin, D. and Heble, A. (eds.) (2004) *The Other Side of Nowhere: Jazz, Improvisation, and Communities in Dialogue*, Middletown, CT: Wesleyan University Press.

Fischlin, D., Heble, A. and Lipsitz, G. (2013) *"The Fierce Urgency of Now": Improvisation, Rights and the Ethics of Co-creation*, Durham, NC: Duke University Press.

Freire, P. (1972) *Pedagogy of the Oppressed*, Harmonsworth: Penguin Education.

Friedman, T. (2006) *The World Is Flat*, London: Penguin Books.

Furlong, J. (2005) 'New labour and teacher education: the end of an era', *Oxford Review of Education*, 31 (1), 119–134.

Galton, M., Simon, B. and Croll, P. (1980) *Inside the Primary Classroom (The ORACLE Report)*, London: Routledge and Kegan Paul.

Gergen, K.J. (2009) *An Invitation to Social Construction*, 2nd ed., London: Sage.

Gergen, K.J. and Gergen, M. (1988) 'Narrative and the self in relationship', in Berkowitz, L. (ed.) *Advances in Experimental and Social Psychology*, New York: Academic Press.

Giddens, A. (1976) *New Rules of Sociological Method: A Positive Critique of Interpretative Methodologies*, London: Hutchinson.

Giddens, A. (1993) *Sociology*, 2nd ed., Cambridge: Polity Press.

Giddens, A. (1999) *Runaway World: How Globalization Is Reshaping Our Lives*, London: Profile.

Gillham, B. (2000) *Case Study Research Methods*, London: Continuum.
Gladwell, M. (2008) *Outliers: the story of success*, London: Penguin.
Glaser, B.G. (1978) *Theoretical Sensitivity: Advances in the Methodology of Grounded Theory*, Mill Valley, CA: The Sociology Press.
Glaser, B.D. (1998) *Doing Grounded Theory: Issues and Discussions*, Mill Valley, CA: Sociology Press.
Glaser, B.G. and Strauss, A.L. (1967) *The Discovery of Grounded Theory: Strategies for Qualitative Research*, Chicago, IL: Aldine.
Goodwyn, A. (2011) *The Expert Teacher of English*, London: Routledge.
Gove, M. (2013) Online. http://www.dailymail.co.uk/debate/article-2298146/I-refuse-surrender-Marxist-teachers-hell-bent-destrog-schools-Education-Secretary-berates-new-enemies-promise-opposing-plans.html [Accessed 10 June 2018]
Grace, G. (2014) 'Professions, sacred and profane: Reflections upon the changing nature of professionalism', in Young, M. and Muller, J. (eds.) *Knowledge, Expertise and the Professions*, London: Routledge.
Grice, H., Hepworth, C., Lauret, M and Padget, M. (2001) *Beginning Ethnic American Literatures*, Manchester: Manchester University Press.
Griffiths, P. (1995) *Modern Music and After: Directions since 1945*, Oxford: Oxford University Press.
Gu, Q. and Day, C. (2013) 'Challenges to teacher resilience: conditions count', *British Educational Research Journal*, 39(1), 22–44.
Habermas, J. (1984) 'The theory of communicative action, Volume 1', *Reason and the Rationalization of Society*. Translated by T. McCarthy. London: Heinemann.
Habermas, J. (1987) 'The theory of communicative action, Volume 2', *The Critique of Functionalist Reason*. Translated by T. McCarthy. Cambridge: Polity Press.
Hairon, S. (2021) 'The emancipatory value of Habermas' critical theory to education'. Available at https://www.encyclopedia.com/education/applied-and-social-sciences-magazines/emancipatory-value-habermas-critical-theory-education [Accessed 25 June 2021].
Hamilton, A (2007) *Lee Konitz: Conversations on the Improviser's Art*, Ann Arbor: University of Michigan Press.
Hanlon, G. (1998) 'Professionalism as enterprise: Service class politics and the redefinition of professionalism', *Sociology*, 32, 42–63.
Hansard (2021) Initial teacher training House of Lords debate, 18 November 2021, Vol. 816. Available at https://hansard.parliament.uk/Lords/2021-11-18/debates/206A9806-1C08-442A-B49A-894ECA06FED2/InitialTeacherTraining?highlight=teacher%20education#contribution-A0A72CC8-E2F9-4DFC-BCAA-A2B7F70B1241 [Accessed 23 November 2021].
Hargreaves, A. and Fullan, M. (2000) 'Mentoring in the new millennium', *Theory Into Practice*, 39 (1).
Hatch, M.J. (1997) 'Jazzing up the theory of organizational improvisation', *Advances in Strategic Management*, 14, 101–191.
Hatch, M.J. (2011) *Organizations: A Very Short Introduction*, Oxford: Oxford University Press.
Hattie, J. (2009) *Visible Learning: A Synthesis of over 800 Meta-analysis Relating to Achievement*, Abingdon: Routledge.
Heidegger, M. (1977) *Basic Writings*, D. Farrell Krell (ed.), New York: Harper and Row.
Hoban, G. (2002) *Teacher Learning for Educational Change*, Buckingham: Open University Press.

hooks, b. (1994) *Teaching to Transgress: Education as the Practice of Freedom*, New York: Routledge.

Hopkins, D. (2000) *After Modern Art 1945–2000*, Oxford: Oxford University Press.

Hopkins, D., Ainscow, M. and West, M. (1994) *School Improvement in an Era of Change*, London: Cassell.

Howell, W. S. (1982) *The empathic communicator*, University of Minnesota: Wadsworth Publishing Company.

Hoyle, E. and John, P. (1995) *Professional Knowledge and Professional Practice*, London: Cassell.

International Commission on the Futures of Education (2020) *Education in a Post COVID World: Nine Ideas for Public Action*. Paris: UNESCO

Johnstone, K. (1979) *Impro: Improvisation and the Theatre*, London: Eyre Methuen.

Jones, L. (1963) *Blues People: Negro Music in White America*, New York: William Morrow.

Joyce, J. (1944) *Stephen Hero*, New York: New Directions Books.

Kandinsky, W. (1977) *Concerning the Spiritual in Art*. Translated from the Russian by M.T.H. Sadler, New York: Dover Publications.

Ko, J., Sammons, P. and Bakkum, L. (2016) *Effective Teaching: A Review of Research and Evidence*, Reading: Educational Development Trust.

Kolb, D. (1984) *Experiential Learning: Experience as the Source of Learning and Development*, Englewood Cliffs, NJ: Prentice Hall.

Kuhn, T.S. (1962) *The Structure of Scientific Revolutions*, Chicago: University of Chicago Press.

Landgraf, E. (2014) *Improvisation as Art: Conceptual Challenges, Historical Perspectives*, London: Bloomsbury.

Lave, J. and Wenger, E. (1991) *Situated Learning: Legitimate Peripheral Participation*, Cambridge: Cambridge University Press.

la Velle, L. (2013) 'Masterliness in the teaching profession: global issues and local developments', *Journal of Education for Teaching*, 39 (1), 2–8.

Leach, J. and Moon, B (1999) *Learners and Pedagogy*, London: Open University.

Levin, B. (1998) 'An epidemic of education policy: (what) can we learn from each other?', *Comparative Education*, 34(2), 131–141, DOI: 10.1080/03050069828234

Levi-Strauss, C. (1966) *The Savage Mind*. Translated from the French by Wiedenfield and Nicolson, London: Wiedenfield and Nicolson.

Lewis, G.E. (2013) 'Critical responses to "theorizing improvisation (musically)"', *Music Theory Online*, 19 (2), June 2013. Available at https://mtosmt.org/issues/mto.13.19.2/mto.13.19.2.lewis.php [Accessed 22 April 2021].

Lincoln, Y.S. and Guba, E. (1985) *Naturalistic Inquiry*, Beverley Hills, CA: Sage.

Lovat, T. (2013) 'Jurgen Habermas: Educations reluctant hero', in Murphy, M. (ed.) *Social Theory and Education Research: Understanding Foucault, Habermas, Bourdieu and Derrida*, London: Routledge: 69–83.

Macey, D. (2000) *Dictionary of Critical Theory*, London: Penguin.

Mackinnon, D. and Statham, J. (1999) *Education in the UK: Facts and Figures*, London: Hodder and Stoughton/Open University

Mearns, I. (2021) *APPG for the Teaching Profession*. Briefing for the Lords' debate on 18th November 2021.

Milton, E., Daly, C., Langdon, F., Palmer, M., Jones, K. and Davies, A.J. (2020) 'Can schools really provide the learning environment that new teachers need? Complexities and implications for professional learning in Wales', *Professional Development in Education*, DOI: 10.1080/19415257.2020.1767177

Mincu, M. and Granata, A. (2021) 'Teachers' informal leadership for equity in France and Italy during the first wave of the education emergency', *Teachers and Teaching*, DOI: 10.1080/13540602.2021.1986695

Mitchell, H. (1997) 'Critical conversation on CPD part two', *CPD Update* 97.

Moss, G., Bradbury, A., Braun, A., Duncan, S. and Levy, R. (2021) *Learning through Disruption: Using Schools' Experiences of COVID to Build a More Resilient Education System*, London: UCL Institute of Education

Nathan, G. (2015) 'A non-essentialist model of culture: implications of identity, agency and structure within multinational/multicultural organizations', *International Journal of Cross Cultural Management* 15, (1), 101–124, DOI: 10.1177/1470595815572171

Newby, P. (2010) *Research Methods for Education*, London: Longman.

Newton, P.M. (2004) 'Leadership lessons from jazz improvisation', *International Journal of Leadership in Education*, 7 (1), 83–99.

Ofsted (2003) *Inspecting Schools: Framework for Inspecting Schools*, London: Ofsted.

Ovenden-Hope, T. (2022) *The Early Career Framework: Origins, Outcomes and Opportunities*, Woodbridge: John Catt Educational Ltd.

Piaget, J. (1951) *The Psychology of Intelligence*, London: Routledge and Kegan Paul.

Piaget, J. (1990) *Childs Conception of the World*, New York: Littlefield Adams.

Plato (1974) *The Republic*. Translated from the Greek by Lee, D. (1974) 2nd ed. Harmondsworth: Penguin Classics.

Plowden, B. (1967) *Children and Their Primary Schools: A Report of the Central Advisory Council for Education*, London: HMSO.

Polyani, M. (1967) *The Tacit Knowledge Dimension*, London: Routledge & Kegan Paul.

Poynton, R. (2013) 'Do improvise: less push', in *More Pause. Better Results: A New Approach to Work (and Life)*, London: The Do Book Company.

Quintilian (1922) *The Insitutio Oraria of Quintilian vol. 4*. Translated from the Latin by H.E. Butler, London: Heinemann.

Rees, S. (1995) 'The fraud and the fiction', in Rees, S. and Rodley, G. (eds.) *The Human Cost of Managerialism*, Sydney: Pluto Press.

Robinson, K. (2010) 'Changing education paradigms' (TED talk). Available at https://www.ted.com/talks/sir_ken_robinson_changing_education_paradigms [Accessed 1 July 2021].

Robinson, K. and Aronica, L. (2015) *Creative Schools: The Grassroots Revolution That's Transforming Education*. London: Penguin.

Robinson, W.L. (1974) 'Conscious competency: the mark of a competent instructor', *Personnel Journal*, 53, 538–539.

Rosch, E. (1973) 'On the internal structure of perceptual semantic categories', in Moore, TE (ed.) *Cognitive Development and the Acquisition of Language*, New York: Academic Press: 112–144.

Rosch, E. (1978) 'Principles of categorisation', in Rosch, E. and Lloyd, B. (eds.) *Cognition and Categorisation*, Hillsdale, NJ: Lawrence Erlbaum.

Rose, S. (2017) *The Lived Experience of Improvisation: In Music, Learning and Life*, Bristol, UK: Intellect.

Rousseau, J.J. (1762) *Emile, or on Education*, London: Penguin Classics.

Rutter, M., Maughan, B., Mortimore, P. and Ouston, J. (1979) *15,000 Hours: Secondary Schools and Their Effects on Children*, Open Books, London.

Ryle, G. (1946) Knowing how and knowing that: the presidential address. *Proceedings of the Aristotelian Society*, 46, new series, 1–16. Retrieved September 2, 2021, from http://www.jstor.org/stable/4544405

Sachs, J. (2001) 'Teacher professional identity: competing discourses, competing outcomes', *Journal of Education Policy*, 16 (2), 149–161.
Santoro, G. (2000) *Myself When I Am Real: The Life and Music of Charles Mingus*, Oxford: Oxford University Press.
Savin-Baden, M. and Major, C. (2013) *Qualitative Research: The Essential Guide to Theory and Practice*, Abingdon: Routledge.
Sawyer, R.K. (2004) 'Improvised Lessons: collaborative discussion in the constructivist classroom', *Training Education* 15 (2).
Sawyer, R.K. (ed.) (2011) *Structure and Improvisation in Creative Teaching*, Cambridge: Cambridge University Press.
Schein, E. H. (2004) *Organizational Culture and Leadership*, 3rd ed., San Francisco: Jossey Bass.
Schön, D. (1983) *The Reflective Practitioner*, New York: Basic Books.
Schwandt, T.A. (2001) *Dictionary of Qualitative Inquiry*, 2nd ed., Thousand Oaks, CA: Sage.
Scott, R. (2014) *Free Improvisation and Nothing: From the Tactics of Escape to a Bastard Science*, ACT – Zeitschrift für Musik & Performance, Ausgabe 2014/5. Available at https://www.act.uni-bayreuth.de/resources/Heft2014-05/ACT2014_05_Scott.pdf [Accessed 6 September 2021].
Seddon, T. (1997) 'Markets and the English: rethinking educational restructuring as institutional design', *British Journal of Sociology of Education* 18 (2), 165–186.
Seidman, S. (1994) *Contested Knowledge: Social Theory Today*, 5th ed., Chichester: Wiley, Blackwell.
Senge, P. (2006) *The Fifth Discipline: The Art and Practice of the Learning Organization*, Revised ed., London: Random House.
Sennett, R. (2008) *The Craftsman*, London: Penguin Books.
Shields, R. (2013) 'Globalisation and the knowledge economy', in Ward, S. ed., *A Students Guide to Educational Studies*, London: Routledge.
Shotter, J. (2008) *Conversational Realities Revisited: Life, Language, Body and World*, Chagrin Falls, OH: Taos Institute Publications.
Shulman, L.S. (1987) 'Knowledge and teaching: foundations of the new reform', *Harvard Educational Review*, 57 (1), 1–21.
Smith, T.W. and Strahan, D. (2004) 'Toward a prototype of expertise in teaching: a descriptive case study', *Journal of Teacher Education*, 55 (4), 357–371.
Snowdon, M. and Halsall, J.P. (eds.) (2019) *Mentorship, Leadership and Research: Their Place within the Social Science Curriculum*, Switzerland: Springer.
Sorensen, N. (1988) *The Value of Improvisation in Arts Education*. MA thesis, Brighton: University of Sussex.
Sorensen, N. (2013) 'The metaphor of the jazz band: ethical issues for leadership', *Critical Studies in Improvisation*, 9 (1). ISSN 1712-0624.
Sorensen, N. (2014) *Improvisation and Teacher Expertise: A Comparative Case Study*. PhD thesis, Bath Spa University. Available at https://www.academia.edu/8108520/Improvisation_and_teacher_expertise_a_comparative_case_study_PhD_final_version
Sorensen, N. (2021a) 'The craft of teaching musical improvisation improvisationally: towards a theoretical framework', in Chapter 16, *The Crafts of Music Education: Reframing Practices and Theory*, Switzerland: Springer Press.
Sorensen, N. (2021b) 'Of course we improvise!' What the best teachers do (and why they do it)', in *Chapter in the Applied Improvisation Mindset*, London: Methuen Drama.
Sorensen, N. (2022) 'Developing the improvising teacher: implications for professionalism and the practice of expertise in improvisation', in *Developing Expertise for Teaching*

in Higher Education: Practical Ideas for Supporting Educational Development, London: Routledge.

Sorensen, N. and Coombs, S. (2010a) 'Whither Postgraduate Professional Development? Towards a theoretical framework to guide long-term teacher development in England', *Professional Development in Education*, 35 (4), 683–689.

Sorensen, N. and Coombs, S. (2010b) 'Authorized to teach?', *CPD Update*, 126 (May 2010), 8–9.

Sorensen, N. and la Velle, L. (2013) 'Catching the sparks: A model of a masters degree in teaching and learning', *Journal of Education for Teaching*, 39(1), 74–92.

Stacey, R.D., Griffin, D and Shaw, P. (2000) *Complexity and Management: Fad or Radical Challenge to Systems Thinking?* London: Routledge.

Stake, R. (1995) *The Art of Case Study Research*, London: Sage.

Sternberg, R.A. and Horvath, J.A. (1995) 'A prototype view of expert teaching', *Educational Researcher*, 24 (6), 9–17.

Stoll, L. (1998) *'School Culture' SIN Research Matters*, London: Institute of Education. No. 9 Autumn 1998.

Stoll, L., Fink, D. and Earl, L. (2003) *It's About Learning (and It's About Time)*, London: RoutledgeFalmer.

Thomas, G. (2011) *How to Do Your Case Study*, London: Sage.

Thomas, G. and James, D. (2006) 'Reinventing grounded theory: Some questions about theory, ground and discovery', *British Educational Research Journal*, 32 (6), 767–795.

Thompson, N. (2016) *The Authentic Leader*, London: Palgrave.

United Nations (2020) Policy brief: Education during COVID-19 and beyond. Available at https://unsdg.un.org/sites/default/files/2020-08/sg_policy_brief_covid-19_and_education_august_2020.pdf [Accessed 23 November 2021].

Van Manen, M. (1977) 'Linking ways of knowing with ways of being practical', *Curriculum Inquiry*, 6 (3), 205–228. Available from http://www.jstor.org/stable/1179579 [Accessed 20 Jan 2014].

Vygotsky, L.S. (1978) *Mind in Society: The Development of Higher Psychological Processes*, Cambridge, MA: Harvard University Press.

Wacquant, L.J.D. (1989) 'Towards a reflexive sociology: A workshop with Pierre Bourdieu', *Sociological Theory*, 7(1), 26–63, DOI: 10.2307/202061

Ward, S. (ed.) (2013) *A Students Guide to Educational Studies*. 3rd ed., London: Routledge.

Warner, S. (2013) *Text and Drugs and Rock and Roll: The Beats and Rock Culture*, London: Bloomsbury.

Wegerif, R. (2008) 'Dialogue or dialectic? The significance of ontological assumptions in research on educational dialogue', *British Educational Research Journal*, 34 (3), 347–361.

Wenger, E. (1998) *Communities of Practice: Learning, Meaning and Identity*, Cambridge: Cambridge University Press.

Whitty, G. (2008) 'Changing modes of teacher professionalism: traditional, managerial, collaborative and democratic', in Cunningham, B. (ed.) *Exploring Professionalism*, London: Institute of Education.

Wilkins, C. (2011) 'Professionalism and the post-performative teacher: new teachers reflect on autonomy and accountability in the English school system', *Professional Development in Education* 37 (3), 389–409.

Williams, R. (1983) *Keywords*, London: Fontana Press.

Winch, C. (2010) *Dimensions of Expertise: A Conceptual Exploration of Vocational Knowledge*, London: Continuum.

Yin, R.K. (2003) *Case Study Research: Design and Methods*, 3rd ed., London: Sage.

Index

Note: **Bold** and *italicized* page numbers refer to figures and tables. Page numbers followed by "n" refer to notes.

accountability 15, 34, 54, 89, 93; discourse of professionalism 57–58; accountability structures 2
adaptation/adaptability 3, 7, 10, 11, 26, 27, 32, 33, 37, 42, 58, 60, 71, 79, 89, 91–93, 96, 99, 101–103, 115, 119, 122, 127, 129, 143
advanced professional practice 2–10, 34–46, 98, 109, 111, 115, 117, 118, 122, 130; development, impact of social culture on 63–76; discourses of 47–60; ecology, grounded theory of 87–90, *88*; lexicon of 34–36; teacher as protype of, improvising 87–97
Advanced Skills Teacher (AST) 57, 102
agency 6, 37, 53, 109, 119, 120, 126, 130, 144; human 17; social 110
Aristotle: 'Art of Poetry, The' 18; *Poetics, The* 8; view of improvisation 18, 21
artful improvisation 19, 91, 96, 122, 130; development of 126–127
artless improvisation 18–19, 28, 96
'Art of Poetry, The' (Aristotle) 18
AST *see* Advanced Skills Teacher (AST)
authenticity 3, 5, 10, 47, 83, 118–121
Authentic Leader, The (Thompson) 119
authoring 5, 10, 118, 120–121
authorisation 3, 5, 10, 47, 120, 121
authorised teacher 5, 10, 118–121, *118*, 130
autonomous professional 50–51; discourse of professionalism 53–54
autonomy 3, 5, 7, 9, 10, 30, 41, 48, 50, 51, 53, 54, 66, 69, 74, 76, 104, 108, 117, 118, 130, 132, 143; professional 5, 109, 116, 144; teacher 3, 9, 72–73, 116, 134

Bakhtin, M. 4, 128
Baraka, A. 22
Barber, M. 116; 'How the World's Best School Systems Stay on Top' 59
Beethoven 19
Benner, P. 38
BERA *see* British Educational Research Association Guidelines (BERA)
'Better Schools: a summary' 52, 56
Black Papers 51
Blake School, The **68**, 69, 70, 77, 80
Braidotti, R. 25
bricolage 23
bricoleur 22–23
Brink, R. 131
British Educational Research Association Guidelines (BERA) 64
Burton, D. 56

Callaghan, J. 51; 'Ruskin' speech 52
Canada: improvisational teaching 3
Capra, F. 66, 99
case study 2, 80–82, 92, 110, 125, 132–134, 138
Chase, W.G. 37
Children and their Primary Schools (Plowden Report) 50
Chomsky, N. 22
classroom culture 80, 82–86, 90, 100, 107
Claxton, G. 23, 28
Coffield, F. 34, 35
cognitive psychology 37, 44
collaborative culture 52
collegial practices 89
collegiate professional 52
Coltrane, J. 22

Index

communicative action 30, 31, 66, 83; theory of 30, 82–83
community 17; of practice 7, 26, 29, 37, 42–45, 55, 66, 74, 79, 92, 96, 121
competence 38; conscious 42; four-stage model of 41–42; levels of 124; professional 55; shared 43; unconscious 39, 42, 46, 117
complex adaptive systems, theory of 32
complexity theory 24, 32, 35
Complex Responsive Processes 32
'Concerning the Spiritual in Art' (Kandinsky) 20–21
connecting 11, 129
conscious competence 42
conscious incompetence 42
content knowledge 117
continuing professional development 2, 4, 6, 31, 51, 121
Coombs, S. 123, **123**
corporal punishment 49
COVID-19 pandemic, improvising teacher during 131–144; face-to-face learning 141–143; innovations in distance learning 133–135; new spaces for learning, creating 138–141; poverty and inequality, addressing 135–136; students' progress, assessing and examining 141; students with special educational needs, supporting 136–138
creativity 3, 16, 21, 24, 26, 27, 47, 72, 73, 108, 116, 126, 144
critical professional learning 117
'critical/self-reflective' form of knowing 30, 31
critical/self-reflective knowledge 104, **105**, 106
critical theory 30, 32, **33**
culture 7, 18, 30, 88, 89, 93, 94, 109–111, 116, 117; classroom 80, 82–86, 90, 100, 107; collaborative 52; definition of 102; of learning 9; organisational 44; pedagogical 132; school *see* school culture; and structure, relationship between 101; target-based 34
curriculum 6, 50, 51, 108, 109; innovation 52; National Curriculum 5, 52

Davies, G. 145n5
deep ecology 25
Delivering World-Class Teacher Development 6
design structures 25, 26, 31, 66, 67, 83, 84, 99, 101, 120

dialogic interaction 27
dialogic practice 90, 115; development of 128
dialogic teaching 7, 9, 60, 80–83, 86, 91, 92, 128
dialogue 4, 11, 23, 31, 34, 80–82, 104, 106, 127, 128
Dickens, C.: *Hard Times* 49
distance learning, innovations in 133–135
Dreyfus, H.L.: theory of expertise 38–42, **39**, 122, 123
Dreyfus, S.L.: theory of expertise 38–42, **39**, 122, 123
Dubin, P. 41
Durant, A. 17; *Improvisation – Arguments after the fact* 16

ecology 9, 10, 29, 89, 92, 97, 98, 144; advanced professional practice, grounded theory of 87–90, *88*; deep 25; school 79, *99*, 109; theory 24
Education Act of 1870 49
'Education Observed 3: Good Teachers' 56
Edward, S. 34, 35
effectiveness 5, 34, 47, 53–59
emergence 24–26, 29
emergent structures 25, 29, 31, 60, 66, 67, 92, 99, 120
emerging professional 49–50
'Emile, or On Education' (Rousseau) 50
emotional intelligence 71
empirical/analytic knowledge 104, **105**
Enlightenment 19–20, 24
equity 31
Eraut, M. 40, 41, 48, 55
Ericsson, K.A. 36, 37
excellence 40
Excellent Teacher 57
exemplary knowledge 64
expertise 6, 7, 34–47, 51, 54, 55, 57, 60, 88, 97, 126, 131; in developing classroom culture 82–86; development of 102, 115, 131; in dialogic teaching 80–82; five-level theory of 122; and improvisation, relationship between 1–3, 10, 28, 63, 77–86, 91–95, **92**; knowledge-based view of 8; non-essentialist view of 90; participants in research 77–78; practice-based view of 8; psychological approach to 37; in relationships 80–82; as social construction 2; social control of 48; sociological approach to 37; teacher perceptions of 77–86; teacher *see* teacher expertise; theories of 8, 38–45

experts: characteristics of 37; definition of 36; knowledge and exceptional performance, relationship between 36–37; performance 8, 35–40, 42, 46, 47, 60, 94; practice 2, 8, 9, 36, 40, 46, 90, 92, 95; teacher *see* expert teacher
expert teacher 9, 45, 65, 67, 70–71, 76, 86, 88, 90, 91, 101, 103; headteachers' perspectives on 70–71; perceptions of 78–80, **79**, **80**; power of 104; shared tendencies of **93**

face-to-face learning 141–143
facticity 119
15,000 hours: secondary schools and their effects on children (Rutter) 53
Fischlin, D. 16, 17
four-phase model of professional practice 4–5
four-stage model of competence 41–42
Freir, P. 128
Fullan, M. 49

generative grammar, theories of 22
generative processes 22–23
Geoffrey Chaucer School, The 77
Gladwell, M. 38
globalisation discourse 58–59
Goodman, R. 56
Gove, M. 5
government policy 7, 101, 108
Grace, G. 47
Granata, A. 134–136, 142, 144
'Great Gatsby, The' 81–82
grounded theory 9, 64, 65, 97, 111, 115; of ecology advanced professional practice 87–90, **88**

Habermas, J. 30–32, 66, 82–83, 94, 99
Hard Times (Dickens) 49
Hargreaves, A. 49
Hatch, M.J. 67
HE *see* higher education (HE)
headteachers perspectives 65–74; on expert teachers 70–71; on improvisation 71–72; on school culture 66–70, **68**; on teacher autonomy 72–73
Heble, A. 16, 17
Heidegger, M.: view of technology 23
Heraclitus 24
Her Majesties Inspectorate (HMI) 52, 56
higher education (HE) 4, 50, 51
historical/hermeneutic knowledge 104, **105**

HMI *see* Her Majesties Inspectorate (HMI)
Hoban, G. 35, 122
Horvath, J.A. 10, 44–45, **45**, 90, 92, 98
Howell, W.S. 41
'How the World's Best School Systems Stay on Top' (Barber and Mourshed) 59
human agency 17

ICFE *see* International Commission on the Futures of Education (ICFE)
improvisation 4, 6–10, 15–33, 40, 46, 47, 60, 64, 67, 75, 76, 90, 96, 104, 109–111, 115, 117, 118–120, 122, **123**, 128, 131, 134, 137, 138, 140, 142–144; Aristotle's view of 18, 21; artful 19, 28, 91, 96, 122, 126–127, 130; artless 18–19, 28, 96; classical references 18–19; definition of 16–17, 25–28, **28**; Enlightenment 19–20; and expertise, relationship between 1–3, 10, 28, 63, 77–86, 91–95, **92**; headteachers' perspectives of 71–72; Kandinsky's view of 20–21, 27; late-modernism 21–22; teacher 1–11; mindset 91, 96, 126, 127, *129*, 130; modernism 20–21; participants in research 77–78; phase of 126; philosophical assumptions of 28–32, 28–33, **33**; post-modern/ecological perspectives of 23–25; practice, characteristics of **25**; pure 26; Quintilian's view of 18–19, 23, 27; research evidence 94–97; romanticism 19–20; skill set 126, 127; structuralism 22–23; and structure, relationship between 99; teacher as expert prototype 90–94; teacher as prototype of advanced professional practice 87–97, **97**; teacher during COVID-19 pandemic 131–144; teacher perceptions of 77–86
improvisational intelligence 28
Improvisation – Arguments after the fact (Durant) 16
inequality 10, 58, 133, 135–136
Initial Teacher Training 6
innovations, in distance learning 133–135
in-service training 51, 52
inspection 7, 35, 57, 58, 67, 69
instrumental virtuosity 21
intelligence 4; emotional 71; improvisational 28
International Commission on the Futures of Education (ICFE) 131
intersubjectivity 4

James Report: *Teacher Education and Training* 50–51
jazz band, the 4, 24–25
Johnstone, K. 27
Joyce, J.: Stephen Hero 20

Kandinsky, W.: 'Concerning the Spiritual in Art' 20–21; view of improvisation 20–21, 27
knowing how to 18, 41, 54, 55, 60, 96, 117
knowing-in-action 55
knowing that 41, 54, 60, 96, 117, 121
knowledge: content 117; craft 63; critical/self-reflective 104, **105**, 106; empirical/analytic 104, **105**; exemplary 64; historical/hermeneutic 104, **105**; pedagogical 117; pedagogical content 117; practical 54, 55; propositional 54; tacit 55
Ko, J. 53
Kolb, D. 55

late-modernism 21–22
Lave, J. 42–44
learner-centred classroom 5, 116, 117, 122, 126
learning identify, constructivist theories of 23
Learning Through Disruption 135, 144
LEAs *see* Local Education Authorities (LEAs)
Levi-Strauss, C. 22, 23
lifeworld 9, 66–67, 69, 74, 76, 82–86, 90, 91, 94, 99, 103, 106, 109, 126; functions of 30–31; at micro level 82–86; structural components of 66–67
Local Education Authorities (LEAs) 50, 52, 56

managerialist discourse of professionalism 56–57
'masterliness' discourse of professionalism: 55–56
Masters in Teaching and Learning (MTL) 55–56
MATS *see* multi-academy trusts (MATS)
McKee, L. 138
McKinsey and Company 59
McKinsey Report 5
Milton Academy, The 68–69
Milton School, The 75
Mincu, M. 134–136, 142, 144
Mingus, C. 98
modernism 20–21; late-modernism 21–22
Morrison, T. 16

Mourshed, M. 116; 'How the World's Best School Systems Stay on Top' 59
Mozart 19
MTL *see* Masters in Teaching and Learning (MTL)
multi-academy trusts (MATS) 5

'Noble Lie' (Plato) 37
non-negotiable design structures 84
noticing 127–128
NQT *see* newly qualified teacher (NQT)

Office for Standards in Education (Ofsted) 35, 57–58, 67
organisational culture 44

Papert, S. 23
paradigm shift 24, 29
pedagogical content knowledge 117
pedagogical culture 132
pedagogical knowledge 117
pedagogy 2–5, 7, 8, 15, 31, 50, 51, 58, 60, 78, 80, 81, 89, 93, 94, 96, 106, 109, 116, 117, 120–122, 125, 128, 132, 138–140; constructivist 4; dialogic 4; metacognitive approaches to 4
performativity agenda 34, 35, 46
permission to improvise 26, 32, 73, 127
personalisation 33, 71, 74, 103, 107, 127
Piaget, J. 4, 50
PISA *see* Programme for International Student Achievement (PISA)
Plato: 'Noble Lie' 37
Plowden Report: *Children and their Primary Schools* 50
PMP *see* professional masters programme (PMP)
Poetics, The (Aristotle) 8
Pollock, J. 21
post-modern/ecological perspectives of improvisation 23–25
poverty 135–136
power 104–109, **105**; relations 32, 44, 95, 96, 98, 105, 106
Poynton, R. 128
practical knowledge 54, 55
prejudice 51
pre-professional stage of professionalism 49
professional autonomy 109, 116, 144
professional competence 55
professional development 3–8, 35, 36, 38, 41, 47, 49, 52, 53, 56, 59, 60, 66, 69, 78, 87, 98, 111, 115–130, 144; adaptation 129; artful improvisation,

developing 126–127; continuing 2, 4, 6, 31, 51, 121; developmental phase of 125; dialogic practice, development of 128; establishment phase of 124–125; improvisational phase of 126; improvisation mindset 127; improvisation skill set 127; of improvising teacher, long-term framework for 114–130; making connections 128–129; noticing 127–128

professionalism 3, 7, 8, 10, 37, 41, 47–60, 115–121, 130; accountability discourse of 57–58; autonomous professional 50–51; autonomous professional discourse of 53–54; collegiate professional 52; effectiveness and 53–59; emerging professional 49–50; fourth professional age 52–53; ideological perspective of 48; managerialist discourse of 56–57; 'masterliness' discourse of 55–56; pre-professional stage of 49; teacher, changing nature of 48–53

professional masters programme (PMP) 4
professional practice 115–118
professional re-evaluation 47
professional relationships 89
professional status 5, 48, 49, 120, 121
Programme for International Student Achievement (PISA) 58–59
propositional knowledge 54
prototype 10, 46, 98, 115; of advanced professional practice, improvising teacher as 87–97; expert teaching **45**; theory 44–45

QTS *see* Qualified Teacher Status (QTS)
Qualified Teacher Status (QTS) 38, 50, 57
Quintilian: view of improvisation 18–19, 23, 27, 96, 122

reflection-in-action 41, 55
reflection-on-action 41, 42, 55
reflective practitioner 41, 54–55, 88
relationships, expertise in 80–82
Revised Code of 1861 49
Robinson, K. 41
romanticism 19–20
Rosch, E. 44–45
Rose, S. 15
Rousseau, J.J.: 'Emile, or On Education' 50
Rutter, M.: *15,000 hours: secondary schools and their effects on children* 53
Ryle, G. 41, 54–55, 96, 117

Sachs, J. 54, 55
SATs *see* standardised assessment tests (SATs)
Scandinavia: improvisational teaching 3
Schein, E. H. 66, 101
Schön, D. 41, 42, 55
school: accountability structures 2; culture *see* school culture; school culture on academic professional practice development, impact of; ecology 79, *99*, 109
school culture 9, 90, 92, 98, *99*, 101–104; definition of 66; impact on expertise practice development 2; model 76
school culture on academic professional practice development, impact of 63–76; data analysis 65; empirical research 63–65; ethical considerations 64–65; headteachers *see* headteachers; interviews with headteachers 65–67; subcultures, importance of 74–76, *75*
School of Artsand Sciences at St. George's University in Grenada, West Indies 134
Seidman, S. 16
self-awareness 20, 70, 119
self-improving school systems 53
self-organisation 24, 29
Shakespeare Academy, The 73, 75, 108
shared competence 43
Shotter, J. 29–30
Simon, H.A. 37
skill acquisition, stages of **39**
Smith, T.W. 92, **93**
social agency 110
social constructionism 29, 32, **33**
social construction of improvising teacher 98–111, *99*; phases of empowerment *110*; power 104–109, **105**; structure 98–101
social justice 30, 31
social nature of learning 4, 84
Sorensen, N. 123, **123**
Stacey, R.D. 24, 79
standardised assessment tests (SATs) 52
Stephen Hero (Joyce) 20
Sternberg, R.A. 10, 44–45, **45**, 90, 92, 98
Strahan, D. 92, **93**
structuralism 22–23
structure 98–101; and culture, relationship between 101; design 25, 26, 31, 66, 83, 84, *99*, 101, 120; emergent 25, 29, 31, 60, 66, 67, 92, *99*, 120
students' progress during COVID-19 pandemic, assessing and examining 141
subcultures 9; importance of 74–76

tacit knowledge 8, 41, 42, 46, 55, 60, 92, 96, 109, 117, 121, 129
teacher: advanced skills 57; autonomy 3, 9, 72–73, 116, 134; during COVID-19 pandemic, improvising 131–144; development, long-term model of 121–124, **123**; effectiveness 54, 59; expertise *see* teacher expertise; as expert prototype, improvising 90–94; improvisation, social construction of 98–111, *99*; leadership 134; non-essentialist view of 10; perceptions of expertise and improvisation 77–86; professionalism, changing nature of 48–53; as professionals 59; as prototype of advanced professional practice, improvising 87–97; quality 3, 6, 7, 34, 52; retention 3, 102
teacher-centred classroom 5, 100, 117, 122
Teacher Education and Training (James Report) 50–51
teacher expertise 1, 3, 8–10, 31, 56, 58, 65, 66, 76, 91, 98, 110, 111, 118, 121; in classroom culture development 82–86; headteachers' perspectives 67–74, **68**; and improvisation, relationship between 63, 77–86, 91–95, **92**; power of 104, 106, 107; in relationships and dialogic teaching 80–82; social construction of 75
teacher–learner relationship 104–105, **105**
Teacher Training Agency 57
Thatcher, M. 52
Thatcherism 52

Thompson, N.: *Authentic Leader, The* 119
TIMMS *see* Trends in Mathematics and Science Studies (TIMMS)
Together Apart Pathways 138–140, *139*
transcendence 119
transformative teleology 32, **33**, 79, 88
Trends in Mathematics and Science Studies (TIMMS) 58–59

UK: advanced professional practice, lexicon of 34–35; Conservative Government 5, 6; Education Act of 1870 49; Education Act of 1902 49; Education Act of 1902 (the Balfour Act) 49; Education Act of 1988 5; Education 'Reform Act' of 1988 52, 56; 'Importance of Teaching, The' 5–6; Masters in Teaching and Learning (MTL) 55–56; National Curriculum 5, 52; secondary schools 2; secondary teachers 2
unconscious competence 39, 42, 46, 117
unconscious incompetence 42
United Nations 131; *Education during COVID-19 and beyond* 132
USA: improvisational teaching 3

vocational commitment to teaching 89, 92

Wenger, E. 42–44
Whitty, G. 48
Williams, R. 17
William Tyndale Affair 51
Winch, C. 40, 41, 44, 45
Wordsworth Academy, The 77

Printed in the United States
by Baker & Taylor Publisher Services